Paul Moore is Vicar of St Wilfri[...] [...]urch near Portsmouth, and a member of the team that launched the first Messy Church in 2004. In addition to being involved in running Messy Church, he has followed the development of Messy Church across the UK and worldwide, with a particular focus on research into the theological and practical aspects of nurturing faith and making disciples. Paul is also a Vocations Adviser for Portsmouth Diocese. When not getting messy, he enjoys listening to progressive rock and playing jazz saxophone.

Written with clarity and conviction, *Making Disciples in Messy Church* is a timely and helpful book for a movement that is deeply serious about discipleship. Drawing on biblical, monastic and catechetical approaches, the book contains much wisdom and inspiration for those seeking to make disciples in all forms of church, not just the phenomenon that is Messy Church. The affirmation of the places of family and community in discipleship formation is especially welcome. I warmly and wholeheartedly commend this book.
Andrew Roberts, Methodist Minister and Director of Training for Fresh Expressions

Discipleship is probably the biggest single issue the Church needs to grapple with in our present times. This book has some vital things to say on this central issue, not only to those interested in Messy Church but to all churches. My advice would be: read it, think about what you read and then apply it in your own situation.
David Male, Director of The Centre for Pioneer Learning, Cambridge

The Messy Church movement is fantastic, helping connect people to Christ and his church through community and creativity. Paul has been on the journey with Messy Church since the start, and in this fascinating book shows how Messy Church is not only reaching people with the Gospel, it is raising up disciples across the world.
Canon Mark Russell, CEO Church Army

Paul Moore writes out of first-hand experience. To this he brings deeper and wider thought. The book brings disparate things together in one place: various frameworks to assess progress in discipleship, lively material from a wide range of Scripture, some ecumenical perspectives and sensible questions to ponder. It ends with solid practical suggestions and knocks on the head the critique that Messy Church has no answers to questions of discipleship. It deserves to be read and applied.
George Lings, Director of The Sheffield Centre

Messy Church® is a registered word mark and the logo is a registered device mark of
The Bible Reading Fellowship

Text copyright © Paul Moore 2013
The author asserts the moral right
to be identified as the author of this work

Published by
The Bible Reading Fellowship
15 The Chambers, Vineyard
Abingdon, OX14 3FE
United Kingdom
Tel: +44 (0)1865 319700
Email: enquiries@brf.org.uk
Website: www.brf.org.uk
BRF is a Registered Charity

ISBN 978 0 85746 218 3
First published 2013
Reprinted 2013
10 9 8 7 6 5 4 3 2 1

Acknowledgments
Page 92: Duncan Macleod's twelve gospel values cited with permission.

Unless otherwise stated, scripture quotations are taken from the HOLY BIBLE, TODAY'S NEW
INTERNATIONAL VERSION®. Copyright © 2001, 2005 by Biblica®. Used by permission of
Biblica®. All rights reserved worldwide. "TNIV" and "Today's New International Version" are
trademarks registered in the United States Patent and Trademark Office by Biblica®. Use of either
trademark requires the permission of Biblica.

A catalogue record for this book is available from the British Library

Printed in Singapore by Craft Print International Ltd

The paper used in the production of this publication was supplied by mills that source their raw
materials from sustainably managed forests. Soy-based inks were used in its printing and the
laminate film is biodegradable.

MAKING
DISCIPLES
IN MESSY CHURCH

Growing faith in an all-age community

Paul Moore

In memory of my mother,
Patricia Moore (1935–2011)

ACKNOWLEDGMENTS

My thanks to the following:

The Diocese of Portsmouth for granting me extended study leave to research this topic.

Ecclesiastical Insurance for a Ministry Bursary Award that enabled me to travel to Australia.

St Wilfrid's, Cowplain, and Westbrook Church for funding my return ticket.

George and Helen Lings for supervision and generous hospitality.

Chris Barnett, Melissa Cellier, Judyth Roberts and the Uniting Church of Australia for inviting us to conferences in Melbourne, Adelaide and Sydney, and all who made us welcome.

The many people from Messy Churches who told me their stories.

Duncan Macleod for fresh insights from the *Mission Stories* programme.

Elizabeth Northcott for taking me up a mountain to see bears, drink coffee and talk about Messy Church.

Lucy Moore for letting me tag along and share in the adventures.

Contents

Foreword

Messy Church is a gift from God, one of the Holy Spirit's wonderful surprises, where a step of faith by one very ordinary church has opened the way for more than a thousand others to engage with families who had no serious connection to a church. No one anticipated that the story publicised in the first Fresh Expressions DVD in 2006 would take on such a life of its own. Messy Church is now a movement in its own right, within the wider Fresh Expressions movement. This book, from Paul Moore, the vicar of that church, presents insights from the oldest member of this young family of churches. They are insights from which all who are committed to disciple-making can benefit.

Those who have been unsure of Messy Church, who would like it to be less messy, and who wonder if it really is church, have frequently raised the question of discipleship. How can you possibly make disciples among all that mess, especially if you meet just once per month? On the contrary, I have always believed that Messy Church is as valid a fresh expression of church as any of the many other models and examples. Because of this, I have always been convinced that the secrets of making disciples through Messy Church lay within the gift itself, in the DNA of the original idea given by the Holy Spirit, and that they would emerge over time. The temptation to bolt on ideas from a different model in order to answer questions or solve apparent problems about disciple-making has always been misguided. It is also evidence of impatience. As the gift of Messy Church has been unwrapped during its early years, the secrets have begun to be revealed.

The Messy Church world is not closed to learning from other sources. Paul draws helpfully from Scripture, from ancient tradition, from other mission practitioners and researchers, from educational theory and from the worldwide Messy family. But, above all, he draws from the underlying values of Messy Church. He tells us not so much how to make disciples through Messy Church as how to create Messy Church as a disciple-making culture, which is much more important.

He sets realistic expectations about the time it takes to journey from no church connection to active faith. He robustly defends intergenerational learning. He wants parents equipped to take responsibility for their children's spiritual development, and team members to see Messy Church as their church, not just the place where they volunteer once a month.

I suspect that there may be even more to be unpacked from this surprising gift over the coming years, but for now this will do very well.

Bishop Graham Cray
Archbishops' Missioner and Leader of the Fresh Expressions Team

'Messy Church needs to reinvent discipleship.'

PAUL BUTLER, BISHOP OF SOUTHWELL

'disciple—to teach, train, educate (obsolete)'

OXFORD ENGLISH DICTIONARY

'The secret was to keep opening doors and to rest with no unanalysed assumptions.'

VINCENT DONOVAN, CHRISTIANITY REDISCOVERED

Introduction

Whether you are just curious about Messy Church, wondering whether to start one up or pondering how to keep one going and growing, I hope this book will help you to reflect on some of the theological and practical issues involved in sharing the good news of Jesus with families and strengthening the Christian faith of children and adults in Messy Church.

We felt we were stepping out in faith into the unknown when we launched the very first Messy Church in April 2004 at St Wilfrid's, Cowplain, a suburban Church of England parish near Portsmouth where I have been the vicar for the last twelve years.

Several of our leaders had been reviewing our work with children and families. We felt frustrated that we were attracting only a handful of children and teenagers on a Sunday morning. Speaking with parents in the school playground, they told us that Sunday morning was a bad time for them to come to anything, let alone a service where children might be expected to sit still and be quiet. At the same time, we realised that quite a number of our church members enjoyed using their creative and artistic gifts. Perhaps God had given us these gifts to use in developing a fresh way of engaging with families in our community.

The seed of an idea sprouted, and the group came up with the simple concept of Messy Church: an hour of Bible-based craft activities (the messier the better) for children and adults to do together, exploring an aspect of the Christian faith, followed by a 15-minute celebration in church, with praise, interactive Bible storytelling, reflection and prayer, and, finally, a sit-down meal in the hall.[1]

A team of crafty people was recruited from our church members. A catering corps was drafted. Paper, paint, glue, scissors, icing sugar and chocolate sprinkles were stockpiled. Invitations went out, largely by word of mouth from our church families to their friends at school.

On the day of the first Messy Church, 90 people turned up, much to our amazement, immediately making this our church's largest congregation. At least half of the families had never been to a service at our church before, except perhaps a school Christmas assembly or a wedding.

The weeks between the monthly sessions seemed to flash by, and families kept coming back and enjoying themselves. In between frantically planning the next session and thinking up new crafts, we began to reflect a bit more on this new thing that God was doing and how best to join in with God and help people move forward in their journey of faith.

If we have any wisdom to offer to the many churches who saw our Messy Church on the first Fresh Expressions DVD, and said, 'We can do that! Let's go for it!' it is still very much wisdom gained on the hoof.[2] We have learnt vast amounts from other people's stories of their Messy Churches, and we have been challenged by the many questions raised—not least this one: 'Is Messy Church making disciples?'

Chapter 1

Is Messy Church making disciples?

Fast-forward to 3.30pm on a September afternoon in 2011. Children with mums, dads and grandparents in tow are arriving at St Wilfrid's for the first Messy Church after the summer holiday. Young and old, newcomers and regulars gather, chat and chill in the church hall over tea, juice and biscuits before we give a welcome and introduce the theme of today's craft activities.

A couple with a young daughter were married in church here last Saturday, and the mother, along with her toddler and the grandmother, has come to Messy Church for the first time today. They have also brought along a cousin and her children. I wonder what impact their experience of Christian community in Messy Church will have on this extended family? Will they be back again next month?

Then in walks a single mum with her daughter. It must be six months since they last came to Messy Church, although we have often waved and shouted 'Hi!' to them across the street on their way to school. 'We've been meaning to come, but just haven't made it,' mum explains as they sign in at the welcome desk.

This particular family has been coming along to Messy Church since we started. They have grown up with us; they belong. I remember when they missed the sixth birthday celebration, they insisted at the next Messy Church that we take down the birthday banner so that they could add their signatures in marker pen alongside all the others. Once a month, Messy Church is their church. They have never attended a Sunday service here, and nobody tries to persuade them that they should do—it might scare them off!

I wonder what impact Messy Church has had on this family? An emotional link with church, a bond, has slowly developed. They are pleased and even proud to have been associated with us for so long, but do they know Jesus better? Have they become Christians? Are they growing as disciples?

I'm sure similar stories could be told from Messy Churches all over the UK and around the world where this fresh way of doing church with families is increasingly being adopted and adapted. Nearly 1,500 Messy Churches have registered on the website (www.messychurch.org.uk/), and many more have not registered yet. Important questions are increasingly being asked by us and by church leaders as to whether people are coming to faith through Messy Church, whether it is making disciples, whether it can justify its claim to be church, or whether it would be better to regard it as a form of pre-evangelism, a bridge to something deeper, perhaps an Alpha course and then graduation to Sunday church attendance.

For those of us putting lots of prayer and hard graft into Messy Church or other fresh expressions of church, these are vitally important questions that we want to take seriously. We need to find reliable answers, so that we can be more effective in what we are doing. At the same time, we need to recognise that these challenging questions are equally urgent and pertinent for traditional or inherited forms of church.

Behind these questions lie certain assumptions that need examining: assumptions about how people come to faith in Christ and what we understand by discipleship. We need to look more closely at what is actually happening in the lives of the adults and children who are coming to Messy

Church. What wisdom can we find in the scriptures, Christian tradition and human experience that can help us in our post-Christendom, postmodern context to present the good news of Jesus and encourage people to respond to God's grace? What examples of good practice can we draw upon from Messy Churches around the world and other forms of church? What needs changing or improving, and what new ideas might merit some experimentation? Hopefully any clues to the answers to these questions will prove helpful not only to Messy Church, but to the whole 'mixed economy' of the Church.

What is happening when people come to Messy Church?

Messy Church aims to be church for non-churched families (those with little or no experience of church), rather than for church families (who turn up regularly), families on the fringe (who turn up occasionally) or de-churched families (who used to come to church services, but stopped, perhaps because they lost the habit when they moved house, fell out with the vicar or had to work on Sundays).

Messy Church began, as we have seen, as a result of our frustration with the lack of young families coming to our Sunday morning 'family service' despite the informal style and well-run junior church groups for children and teenagers. If families would not come to us, perhaps we should be taking steps towards them. Conversations with some of the families in our local community about the kind of church activity they would like to attend led to a consensus that a monthly, fun, craft-based event for families, not on a Sunday, would fit the bill.

Our Messy Church meets once a month on a Thursday afternoon after school. Many Messy Churches meet midweek like ours, while others find Sunday afternoon is a good time for families, and some choose Saturday. Before deciding what to do and when, it is essential to do your research properly and listen to those you are hoping to reach.

Typical attendance at our Messy Church in Cowplain is around 80 adults and children, although the numbers fluctuate, depending on whether there is something on at one of the local schools, such as a disco or a school play. This total figure of 80 includes the team running the crafts and cooking the meal. The team is made up of about 20 adults and teenagers, who are mostly, but not exclusively, drawn from our committed church families. Of the remaining 60 adults and children, just over half do not attend church at any other time. The rest are families who come to St Wilfrid's on Sunday or belong to other local churches, but see Messy Church as providing something extra for their family.

So a significant proportion of those who regularly attend our Messy Church are adults and children with little or no church background. Our prayer is that through their monthly experience of Christian community in Messy Church, they will receive God's **blessing**, and, through this experience of **belonging**, will come to **believe** in and follow Christ, learning to **behave** as Christian disciples who bring God's blessing to others.

It is vital that we give families a warm welcome at the 'blessing' entry point into this cycle (shown in the diagram below) and do all we can to help them develop a sense of belonging to Messy Church over the first few months. As they progress through the stages of this cycle, they will need different input, support and encouragement at each stage to keep them moving on towards believing, behaving and blessing others. Assuming they complete the cycle, those who have become followers of Jesus should in theory continue on a spiral of ever-deeper fellowship, faith and love of God and neighbour—without falling off or getting stuck.

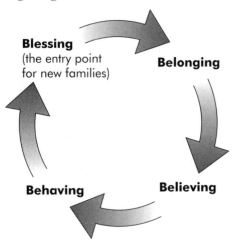

Blessing
(the entry point for new families)

Belonging

Behaving

Believing

Judging by the stories from Messy Churches in the UK and elsewhere, encouraging numbers of non-churched people are reaching the 'believing' stage, coming to faith in Jesus Christ and going on to grow as disciples. This has resulted in a number of Messy baptisms in various places, and what was probably the first Messy confirmation service in Derby.

The long and winding road

Jo Gill of Marshalswick Baptist Free Church in St Albans, writing on the Messy Church blog, tells the story of a man who was brought to church by his girlfriend's grandma to help out on one of the craft tables:

He had no background of church and was quite nonplussed by Christianity when he first came… He was not interested in church but was willing to get involved… He came along and then wanted to help again. We then started the Journeys course and he decided to come along. He was a bit into space life and belief in other things out there… not sure what, but couldn't grasp Christianity. He is now wanting baptism.[3]

There are several points of interest in this man's story. First, he had no church background. He was indifferent to church and puzzled by Christian beliefs, but he still had his own thoughts and beliefs about the spiritual dimension of life. Research suggests this would be fairly typical of non-churched adults in the UK.[4] It would equate to about −7 on the Engel Scale, a tool developed by James Engel in the 1970s to show the spectrum of spiritual knowledge and awareness from 'no real awareness of God' at −7 through to growth in Christ at +4 (see the diagram on page 20).[5]

Spiritual awareness

4	Growth in Christ
3	Conceptual and behavioural growth
2	Incorporation into body
1	Post-decision evaluation
−1	Repentance and faith in Christ
−2	Personal problem recognition
−3	Grasp of implications of gospel
−4	Awareness of basics of gospel
−5	Initial awareness of gospel
−6	Awareness of true God
−7	No real awareness

No knowledge

The Engel Scale

The Engel Scale is only a rough guide, but it can be useful to help us assess where people are spiritually, so that we can have some idea of the next step they need to take towards faith in Christ and offer appropriate help. It also reminds us that coming to faith and becoming a disciple is one long process that takes a lifetime.

Evangelism is the first stage in making disciples. We turn afresh to Christ each day, and someone who became a Christian years ago is on the same journey towards God as those who are just starting out. We need to remember when recording our church attendance statistics that Jesus commands us to make obedient disciples, not 'average weekly attenders'.

If we have not yet seen vast crowds of people becoming Christians and advancing in discipleship through Messy Church, this does not necessarily mean God is not working in people's lives. There are plenty of encouraging stories to tell of people attending Messy Church who have moved several points up the Engel Scale. There's the dad who always used to wait outside in the car to collect his child, but now comes in for a coffee and a chat. Or there's the atheist husband of a Messy Church leader who now helps clear up after the craft session and sets the tables for the meal. Both these men have probably moved from –7 to –5 on the scale over a period of months, which is significant progress. With prayer and gentle encouragement they may take further steps towards faith.

What John Finney observed some years ago while he was Church of England Officer for the Decade of Evangelism remains true: for most people the journey towards a committed and owned faith in Christ usually takes between one and five years, sometimes longer.[6] If your Messy Church has been going for only a few months or even a couple of years, do not lose heart if you have not seen revival break out. At this relatively early stage it is unrealistic and unfair to expect you to be able to produce figures for the number of people who have become Christians as evidence of the effectiveness of this work. Of course God can, and often does, wonderfully surprise us with encouraging exceptions to the norm when certain people seem to be on a fast-track to faith, but even in these cases God has often been patiently at work in their lives over many years.

This has important implications, therefore, for how a Messy Church is evaluated by its leadership team and by church councils, ministers and denominations, especially when there are decisions to be made about staffing and funding. Just as the plum tree my wife Lucy planted in our garden will need several years to establish itself and grow before we can expect it to produce a crop of more than one or two tiny plums, so a new Messy Church will require investment in leaders and resources for far longer than just a couple of years if it is to have a proper chance of producing Christian disciples.

Returning to the story of the man who came along to help out, came to faith and was baptised, it is obvious, but worth noting, that he would probably never have come had someone not brought him along and given him a job to do. Personal invitation and being brought along by someone you know and trust are vital for introducing people into an alien environment, whether it is church or the local bowls club. Publicity does sometimes bring people in off the street, but it is no substitute for networking and building relationships with people.

As in this man's story, encouraging newcomers to take on tasks and responsibilities is an important strategy to adopt, because they then feel needed. This reinforces their sense of belonging and the feeling that they are contributing to Messy Church rather than having something done to them or for them.

Those attending this particular Messy Church were offered the chance to supplement the monthly meeting by joining the Journeys course, which was then followed by Christianity Explored. Journeys is a DVD-based course developed in New Zealand for those who are not yet ready for Alpha. It is good to see more resources of this type appearing, specifically designed for people at the lower end of the Engel Scale who have some interest in the spiritual dimension of life but little or no knowledge of Christianity. This is the case for many of the people we are welcoming to Messy Church. We need good introductory resources like these, not only so that courses can be offered alongside Messy Church, but also so that we can learn from them and develop ideas for exploring faith more effectively in Messy Church sessions.

Most of these courses, not surprisingly, bear a strong family resemblance to the proven formula of Alpha and are aimed at adults. I have not yet come across any similar materials specifically designed for use by adults and children together in an all-age context like Messy Church or in the family home, and I think we need this kind of material.[7]

The Gray Matrix

So far we have used the Engel Scale to think about where people coming to Messy Church are on a journey towards

Christian faith and discipleship. The Gray Matrix, developed by Frank Gray of the Far East Broadcasting Company (FEBC), is an extremely helpful modification of the Engel Scale.[8] Gray adds a second, horizontal, axis, which is a spectrum of feeling and attitude towards Christian faith and church, showing how closed or open a person is to the gospel. This enables us to take into account what an individual's feelings are about God and the gospel as well as their level of knowledge about the Christian faith. Are they antagonistic or enthusiastic? Gray also suggests we keep in mind a third invisible dimension, an axis going through the centre, which represents the work of the Holy Spirit in a person's life (see the diagram opposite).

Plotting where our Messy Church families might be on this diagram can be revealing. If, for ease of reference, we number the quadrants clockwise from 1 to 4, then families in our Messy Church who already have links with church and a positive, open attitude to Christian beliefs and the church would be placed somewhere in quadrant 1 (say +3, +3).

Those with little or no church background, such as the man dragged along to Messy Church to help with the crafts, would be found in quadrant 3 (say –3, –7). They may have little knowledge of what Christians really believe and all manner of negative feelings about God and the church.

I would describe quadrant 3 as the **Friendship Quadrant**. This is because, if we want to help people in this quadrant come closer to God, we will need to channel our energies and plan our programmes in such a way as to build relationships of trust with these non-churched people. By giving them a positive experience of Christian community through our welcome,

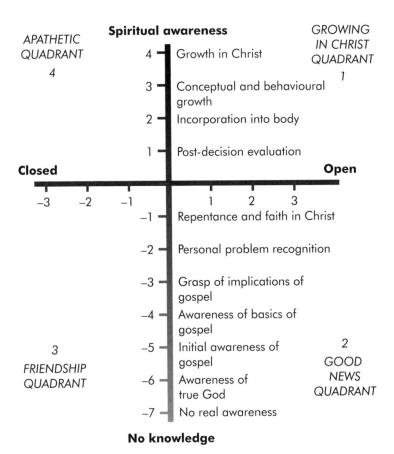

APATHETIC QUADRANT 4

Spiritual awareness

GROWING IN CHRIST QUADRANT 1

4 — Growth in Christ

3 — Conceptual and behavioural growth

2 — Incorporation into body

1 — Post-decision evaluation

Closed

Open

−3 −2 −1   1 2 3

−1 — Repentance and faith in Christ

−2 — Personal problem recognition

−3 — Grasp of implications of gospel

−4 — Awareness of basics of gospel

−5 — Initial awareness of gospel

3 FRIENDSHIP QUADRANT

−6 — Awareness of true God

2 GOOD NEWS QUADRANT

−7 — No real awareness

No knowledge

hospitality, generosity and love, they should begin to lose their negative attitudes arising from misconceptions about the Christian faith or bad experiences of church in the past.

The fact that the man who helped out was keen to come again means that God was using something in his experience of Messy Church to change his view of the church and faith.

Was it the welcome, the conversations, making friends, the fun and laughter of getting messy, the feeling of being useful, the celebratory worship and prayer, the shared meal, or a Spirit-empowered combination of all of these factors? Certainly, over the months, he was gradually shifting in his attitude and feelings, moving towards quadrant 2, towards a more open, positive interest in Christian faith (say +1, −7).

Quadrant 2 can be described as the **Good News Quadrant**, because people here are more open and receptive to the gospel than those in quadrant 3. They will require a different approach and emphasis. They need to be given opportunities and permission to ask all sorts of questions, maybe joining a course like Journeys. If they continue to be open and interested, then it will be important for them to be made aware of the cost of following Jesus, to have the chance to talk all this through with a Christian friend, and, at the right moment, to be helped to take their first steps of faith before marking in some clear way (by baptism, where appropriate) their arrival at a committed personal faith.

So far the man's faith journey has taken him from the Friendship Quadrant (3) to the point in the Good News Quadrant (2) where he is open and interested enough to join the Journeys course (+2, −5), followed by Christianity Explored. He hears and grasps the good news of Jesus, believes it for himself (+2, −1) and as an enthusiastic new Christian enters quadrant 1 when he gets baptised (+3, +2).

Quadrant 1 could be called the **Growing in Christ Quadrant**, because this is where the lifelong process of learning to live as a disciple should begin and continue.

Reflecting on this quadrant, it seems to me that the church's record on making disciples is at best patchy.[9] I was brought up in a rural Anglican church where preparation for confirmation as a young teenager was effectively the end of one's adult Christian formation. Many of my contemporaries clearly felt this to be so, because after their confirmation they never appeared in church again. If you did keep coming, you were expected to keep your faith going on your own, sustained by Sunday worship, receiving Holy Communion, digesting sermons and sometimes taking part in a Lent study course, if you were really keen.

Of course, much has changed for the better since then. We have recognised the importance for faith development and discipleship of encouraging people to meet regularly in smaller fellowship groups or house groups (as in the early church and the Methodist movement), and we have seen the popularity and effectiveness of food-and-faith discussion-based courses like Alpha. There is still a danger, though, that if we fail to provide fledgling Christians with the right learning environment, opportunities and support for their growth in Christ and daily living for God, then, sadly, like many churchgoers, they may never advance much beyond (+3, +1). They may never feel much connection between their faith and daily life. Faith remains largely theoretical and private, and gives them little hope or motivation. Eventually, as they face the normal hardships of life, they may become disillusioned and disappointed with their experience of church and its lack of impact on the rest of the week. Imperceptibly they can drift into quadrant 4, where faith becomes lukewarm and church becomes a duty and a chore. This quadrant could be called the **Apathetic Quadrant**, and it is not far from the door marked 'exit'.

The Gray Matrix is a useful tool, reminding us that evangelism is about winning hearts as well as minds. Certainly Messy Church has proved itself to be good at winning hearts, building friendships and altering attitudes to church.

Just coming into a church building for the first time can be daunting for non-churched families. Messy Church is right, therefore, to put a lot of effort into the warm welcome, generous hospitality, fun, friendship and gentle, exploratory, no-strings-attached spirituality for families who tend to come with a postmodern suspicion of the church as a source of authority. Because their children enjoy themselves, parents are keen to bring them every month, though they would be reluctant to attend a traditional church service.

Talking to families at our Messy Church, attitudes typical of the Friendship Quadrant (3) in the Gray Matrix are often revealed as parents express their ambivalent attitude to church and religion. Adults can seem quite defensive at first, presumably because in our culture an interest in religion is felt to be childish or embarrassing to admit to in conversation. 'We don't do God,' as Alastair Campbell, former Press Secretary to Tony Blair, once said. Blair himself has admitted he was reticent about his faith while Prime Minister, because he might have come across as 'a nutter'. Even people of faith are anxious not to appear strange. One mum at our Messy Church commented, 'You don't have to be religious to come; we're not.' But experience of Messy Church's creative and exploratory approach over the months does seem to lead to a more open and positive attitude. 'You're not preached at, but the godly theme is there, it's underlying,' said another mum. They appreciate the feeling of community, and express their preference for this form of church to others they have experienced: 'This shakes off the image of what people think church is like,' said one of our dads. 'My kids would rather come here than to a birthday party.'[10]

Stories from other Messy Churches suggest that the eagerness of the children is often the reason why families keep coming. The children's engagement is clearly often deeper than having fun, because it is often children who begin conversations about the Bible theme over the meal or insist on acting the story out again at home. Jane Leadbetter, who leads the L19 Messy Church in Liverpool, describes how, during the first course of the meal, children and adults at the tables are encouraged to chat about four or five 'wondering questions' related to the day's theme:

After doing this for a few months I have noticed how the children want to read the questions and lead the answering. Some children now ask for a pencil and try to write down their answers. This last month a child asked me for more questions. I really feel that the children are leading this forward and I am excited about how it may develop.

In March we had Messy Saints as our Messy Church fell on St Patrick's Day. In the celebration time in church we acted out the story of St Patrick, big style, with props and loud noises. A young boy of around seven years of age volunteered to be St Patrick. I sat down at his table to engage with the 'I wonder' questions and enjoy a meal. He was with his mother, brother, an aunt and a cousin. We do not see them in Sunday church. As he tried to read out the questions the young boy started to take us right through the St Patrick story. Neither of the adults interrupted him, and at the end he said, 'and that is why St Patrick was a Christian and he wants everyone to trust God too'. I gulped and realised that by taking part in the drama he had grasped not only the story but also the language used by the storyteller, and he declared it without a doubt... The family come to every Messy Church now, and the mother has asked to be in the Messy team on a craft table.[11]

What stories like this reveal is that children at Messy Church may often be leading their parents and other family members on the faith journey, which is an interesting dynamic that merits further research and reflection.

Messy Church aims to reach whole families with the love of God. Children are not dropped off at the door. They must be accompanied by an adult, usually mum, often granny or a childminder, less often dad or both parents together. Research by Judy Paulsen at her Messy Church just outside Toronto in Canada confirms that Messy Church is good at helping parents to become more open and talk about church and faith with their children. Interestingly, for a quarter of their families the accompanying adult is the grandmother and the parents have no church contact.[12] I can think of several similar families in our Messy Church. One grandmother brings her granddaughters every month and attends Sunday church herself every week, while mum and dad are agnostic or atheist and do not come. We hope and pray that the girls' positive experience of Messy Church has an impact on the parents, gradually changing their perception and attitudes, and that they will eventually come into the Friendship Quadrant because of their children's enthusiastic witness.

Attitudes of children and adults towards church and faith are being changed at Messy Church through their experience of Christian community. Families are gradually journeying towards the Good News Quadrant ($+1$, -5). They are becoming more open to the gospel, and will no doubt be watching very carefully to see what difference faith makes in the lives of the Christians on the Messy Church team. If they become friends with Christians, they will be able to see what faith and discipleship are. To help them progress further, each new family probably needs to forge a strong friendship with at least one Christian adult and ideally with a Christian family with children of a similar age. Of course this raises big issues around the time and commitment required from members of the team, and how we need to inspire, train and encourage our church families to befriend non-churched families.

Using the Gray Matrix to see the many different stages people attending Messy Church are at in their faith journey can help the leaders to see more clearly what they need to provide to enable adults and children to continue moving forward, and also what kinds of input and support they need to plan and make provision for in the future. If it is the case that in many families the children are more open to the gospel than their parents, and mum, dad and grandma are all at different places on the Gray Matrix, how can Messy Church effectively assist the whole family? We find ourselves needing to do pre-evangelism, evangelism and discipleship work all at the same time. No wonder this is challenging and messy!

At least the Gray Matrix gives us a map to help us see the different points people are at on their exodus-like journey of faith, where they should be heading next, and how we can accompany and encourage them in moving forward. The probable route is shown in the following diagram.

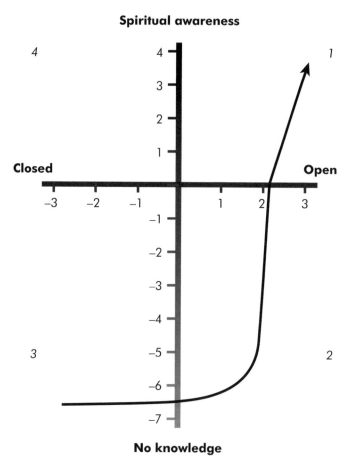

Spiritual awareness

No knowledge

The Messy journey into discipleship

Frank Gray makes the point that if a church intends to make disciples of people who are on this journey, then it needs to examine its programme and ensure that it is providing appropriate activities to move people onwards at all stages of the route. To do all of this in one monthly Messy Church meeting is a huge challenge. Getting it anywhere near right will require a willingness to experiment and make changes. If, after time, we see evidence that people at different points are progressing onwards and upwards, then our approach is clearly working. At all times we need to engage with both knowledge and attitude, head and heart, and cooperate with the way the wind of God's Spirit is blowing in the all-important but unseen third dimension.

First we need to facilitate more openness through positive experiences of Christian community and building relationships and trust. There are subsequent stages in which we gradually introduce people to Jesus and the gospel, help them to take their first steps of faith and provide the right learning environment for lifelong growth in discipleship.

How can Messy Church (or any church) do all these things equally well? Churches are likely to be better at one or more aspects and adequate or failing in others. It seems to me that Messy Church is more effective than many forms of church in helping people to progress towards greater openness and begin climbing the upward curve. The emphasis on welcome, community, friendship and unpressured exploration seems to be an important factor in this. Significant numbers of people are arriving at the Growing in Christ Quadrant (1) as a result, and there is now an urgent need to address their onward journey as disciples.

What does Messy discipleship look like? How do we make disciples in today's messy context? We want to draw upon the wisdom of scripture and our Christian heritage, while also recognising that we are entering unfamiliar territory. In the words of Bishop Paul Butler, 'Messy Church needs to reinvent discipleship.'[13]

For further thought and discussion:

✣ What does your church programme provide to help people who are at different stages of the journey into faith and discipleship?
✣ Where are the gaps or weaker aspects, and what could be done to improve things?

Chapter 2

What are disciples and how are they made?

New inventions are often inspired by the rediscovery of an old idea. If we are to reinvent discipleship, we need to look to the scriptures and Christian tradition, asking what a Christian disciple is (the concept) and looking for clues as to how disciples are made (the process). It is also helpful to reflect on how people acquire knowledge, beliefs, values, skills and behaviours, drawing on insights from learning theory, and in particular the relationships between the three types of learning illustrated in the triangular diagram below.[14]

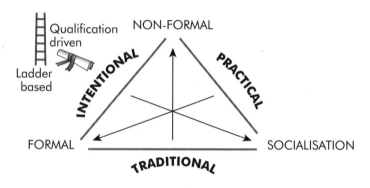

N.B. Jesus used all three. All have their place, but deliver different things best.

How do children learn to speak their mother tongue? Not by attending classes or buying a DVD course advertised in the Sunday newspaper. Small children pick it up gradually through listening and imitation. From the child's perspective, the process is not intentional; it happens naturally as part of the child's mental and physical development. This is a process of socialisation (at the right-hand corner of the triangle), and has practical and traditional aspects.

Later, at school or college, the same person may study a second language or perhaps linguistics (the morphology and grammar of language), and this process will be intentional, formal, rational, conceptual and academically driven, with less of a practical element. This is formal learning (the left-hand corner of the triangle), which has both intentional and traditional aspects.

The third mode of learning (at the apex of the triangle) is non-formal. An example would be an apprentice carpenter who acquires a set of skills by working and learning alongside a master carpenter. While there are undoubtedly traditional elements in learning a trade such as carpentry, this is essentially learning on the job, both intentional and practical. Interestingly, non-formal learning has been demonstrated to be less likely to reinforce norms and traditions than socialisation. In other words, it is more open to new possibilities.

Bob Hopkins, a member of the Fresh Expressions team, has used this model of learning types to reflect on the way clergy and church leaders are trained for ministry. Usually ministers are required to complete several years of theological training, attending lectures, reading, writing assignments and sitting exams. This largely formal mode of learning, with its emphasis on tradition, tends therefore to produce church leaders who reinforce existing patterns of ministry and inherited modes of church, which may not be what the church actually needs.

Hopkins argues that if we want to train and equip future church leaders for new forms of pioneer ministry, fresh expressions of church, like Messy Church, and innovative outreach work, then alongside academic learning there needs to be a greater emphasis on the other two modes of learning. We should encourage more non-formal training in the shape of apprenticeships alongside effective leaders, and more socialisation using placements in missional churches (where there is a strong ethos that every member is sent out by God to make a difference in his or her daily life). This should produce ministers who can adapt more easily and effectively to new situations. Similarly, I would argue that local churches need to be using all three modes of learning to make disciples who will be able to adapt to living as Christians in our ever more rapidly changing world.

When we hear the word 'teaching' used in church circles, what does it usually refer to? It might be used to describe the preaching of sound biblical doctrine from the pulpit week by week, or perhaps that special form of instruction for which the children go out to Sunday school.

How often do we hear the word 'learning' used in church, apart from when we are coaxed into learning a new hymn tune or worship song? Most of the regular teaching in our churches, however well prepared and presented it may be, is more formal and traditional than practical and motivational. In fact, what is urgently required is more non-formal, intentional, practical learning combined with socialisation in a church community where together we can get to grips with the expectation that Christians should live out their faith in daily life.

Learning to be a disciple is rather like learning to play a musical instrument. Lectures and books are unlikely to be much help or encouragement, especially in the early stages.

What is required first and foremost is an immersive learning experience involving socialisation and non-formal learning through observation, imitation, experiment and many hours of practice, so that the skills required become second nature. Orchestral players and choir members also have to learn through experience how to play and sing in time and in tune with others, and likewise members of a church have to learn to cooperate with each other and with the Holy Spirit to achieve the harmony, or unity in diversity, that should characterise the body of Christ.[15]

In rethinking disciple-making in the community of the church and the family, it is important to recognise that socialisation is not necessarily an accidental and haphazard process. More often than not it has an intentional element behind it. We see this, for example, when bilingual parents decide to speak both French and English in the family home so that their children grow up to be bilingual too; or when mum and dad agree never to argue in front of the children, or decide not to allow their children to use the internet or have a television in their bedroom. Ways of behaving based on underlying values and beliefs are being learnt and reinforced through socialisation in every family and community, for good or ill. It is therefore essential that we consider the various decisions and perhaps unspoken values that lie behind the way we expect people to belong, believe and behave within our church communities.

Bearing all three modes of learning in mind—formal, non-formal and socialisation—we turn next to the scriptures to see what we can discern about disciple-making from the various parts of the biblical record.

For further thought and discussion:

✤ How have the three modes of learning contributed to your growth as a Christian? Which do you think is the most significant?

✤ To what extent does your church provide an immersive learning experience, paying attention to non-formal learning and socialisation?

Chapter 3

Old Testament discipleship

It might seem a little perverse to begin with the Old Testament, which obviously does not describe Christian discipleship. However, to omit the Hebrew scriptures would be to lose a sense of the big story, or metanarrative, of the Bible concerning God's mission of love to renew creation and reconcile all things in Christ. Making disciples is a vital part of God's mission in which we are invited to join.[16] The Old Testament points to and prepares the way for Christ, and discipleship themes are pre-echoed in the stories of the patriarchs and God's chosen people.

Abraham and Sarah —prototype disciples?

Abraham and Sarah are arguably the prototypes for all disciples. The apostle Paul says that Abraham is 'the father of all who believe', from whatever background (Romans 4:11–12, 16–17). Abraham and Sarah are chosen by God and called to set off on a journey to a new land, trusting God's promise that 'all peoples on earth will be blessed through you' (Genesis 12:1–3).

Discipleship begins with God's gracious call. Abraham is chosen for the job, but as a wealthy moon-god worshipper he is far from being a perfect candidate, particularly since he and Sarah have no children and time is running out. Yet God enters into a binding covenant relationship with them. Like Abraham and Sarah, disciples of Christ are chosen by God's sovereign will, not because of any merit they have in themselves. Through

God's grace they are called into a covenant relationship and sent out on his mission to the world.

Abraham responded to God's call. He left, he obeyed (Genesis 12:4), because he believed and trusted God's promise sufficiently to set out in faith. This is a picture of the defining moment in which a person becomes a disciple by making an initial response of faith and trust to God's call and promise. This moment sets every disciple on a new course through life under God's direction.

As Abraham and Sarah's discipleship journey unfolds, we see God testing and training their trust and obedience through various trials and troubles, often of their own making. Their faith wavers. Their doubts and fears lead them to make wrong decisions which have serious and near-disastrous consequences. Abraham twice pretends that Sarah is his sister, and agrees to her suggestion that he should father a son with her maid Hagar, but God prevents them from derailing his plan, and through all these experiences Abraham's faith grows. Eventually the promised son Isaac is born.

Then comes the ultimate test of faith, when God commands Abraham to offer this beloved son as a sacrifice. Will Abraham obey God's order and kill the son of the promise? He binds and lays Isaac on the altar. He raises the knife. At that moment the test is suddenly halted. There is no need to continue because, the angel of the Lord says, 'Now I know that you fear God' (Genesis 22:12).

Like Abraham, our father in faith, all disciples are being schooled in 'the fear of the Lord', refined in the crucible of experience, having our faith and trust in God's promises exercised and strengthened. Much of the time this process takes place largely unnoticed by us, like the socialisation of children within a family, but this is how God intentionally makes disciples through lifelong learning. (See, for example, Romans 5:3–5 on the positive outcomes of suffering and Hebrews 12:7–11 on the fruits of God's discipline in our lives.)

Abraham and Sarah are encouraging archetypes for discipleship, because they are far from perfect, yet God patiently persists with them. This is neither formal theological education nor a basics course like Alpha. This is learning about God and learning to trust him through the ups and downs of life—a totally immersive learning experience that takes a lifetime and requires grace, trust, hope, patience and perseverance.

The same kind of messy discipleship process can be seen in the faith journeys of the generations that follow Abraham and Sarah, in the stories of Isaac, Jacob and sons, and Moses.

God's chosen people —an experiment in community discipleship

Having chosen Abraham to be the father of many nations (Genesis 17:4), several generations later God keeps the promise alive when he saves Jacob's family from starvation by sending Joseph ahead of them to Egypt. The 70 descendants of Jacob (Exodus 1:5) are fruitful and multiply into a great tribe of

Hebrews who eventually become slaves under the oppressive rule of a new pharaoh.

It is at this point, with Moses and the exodus story, that the themes of discipleship in the Old Testament widen from the individual to the community level. God steps in again to rescue a people whom he has graciously chosen for his own. Having called them and brought them out of Egypt, he enters into a covenant relationship with them at Sinai, giving them the Law as their guide for living as his holy people, a community of grace, blessing and promise.

Looking back to the three types of learning, the giving of the Law is obviously an example of formal learning, which is both intentional and traditional. Yet God's Law is also going to provide a practical test of the people's trust and obedience in the years ahead, just as Abraham's great trial did earlier.

As the story continues, God begins to test and refine their faith non-formally in the crucible of their wilderness experiences of hardship, so that they will be able to carry forward his promise and his mission to the nations. As with the patriarchs, this proves to be a long process, with many setbacks and failures along the way due to the people's lack of faith.

The pattern continues when, eventually, they enter the land and settle; generations pass and they manage to lose the book of the Law. Their distinctive values and behaviour as God's people are eroded by the influences of the pagan nations around them, just as Moses had warned. Their trust and obedience steadily decline, despite the dire warnings of the prophets. God's judgment falls first on Israel, then Judah is also conquered, and the exile begins. However, the prophets remain aware that the Lord in his mercy is still patiently shaping his people for the future fulfilment of the promise and the mission.

The Old Testament describes how God's people were instructed to remember and build up their faith and obedience, and pass on to the next generation the call to be a holy people. This was a programme for the intentional socialisation of God's people into a behavioural tradition for generations to come, so that they would 'walk in obedience to the Lord' (see Deuteronomy 5:23, 10:12, 11:22, etc.). Their story and status were to be recalled and celebrated by everyone at the seven great annual festivals of Passover, Unleavened Bread, First Fruits, the Feast of Weeks (Pentecost), the Feast of Trumpets, the Day of Atonement and the Feast of Booths (Tabernacles or Ingathering). These festivals were communal, all-age worship events drawing together the whole people of God to commemorate and keep alive the story of what God had done for his people, and to renew their commitment to God's Law and promise—to living as his people.

As well as these major celebrations, there were smaller gatherings of the extended family for the weekly observance of the Sabbath. Families were instructed to keep remembering and discussing the Lord's commandments when going about their everyday lives, 'when you sit at home and when you walk along the road, when you lie down and when you get up', lest they forget (Deuteronomy 6:6–10; 11:19–21). Lifelong discipleship—walking in the way of the Lord (Judges 2:22)—was to be maintained and developed through gathered community celebrations and extended family cells. Notice the all-age emphasis of both. Belief and behaviour were nurtured with all generations together at both festival and family level. How do we expect to pass our faith on from one generation to another if we usually split the generations up for 'age-appropriate' teaching?

I suppose one could argue that the Old Testament story demonstrates how ineffective these disciple-making methods were, because the people so rapidly and repeatedly turned away from God. However, recalling G.K. Chesterton's comment that 'the Christian ideal has not been tried and found wanting; it has been found difficult and left untried' (*What's Wrong with the World*, 1900), I wonder whether the heart of the discipleship problem in Israel and Judah may simply have been that God's people did not do as they had been told. They failed to keep the tradition alive, or at least failed to keep its true purpose in mind. The festivals became riddled with pagan practices or were discontinued. Chatting informally about God in everyday life was replaced by phylacteries, rituals and Pharisaical arguments about precisely what you could or should not do on the Sabbath.

Perhaps there is wisdom to be found here on how we can make disciples in Messy Church by developing an intentional socialisation programme. By celebrating the great things God has done for us in Christ through imaginative, participative all-age celebrations and feasting at major festivals of the Christian calendar, God's people can learn to live in a rhythm of reviewing, renewing and passing on their faith. Alongside these big celebrations, families need help to develop a weekly

Sabbath rhythm, as well as the heartbeat of faith at home and in all aspects of daily life.

Most Messy Churches meet once a month with a break for the summer holidays, so we already have eleven potential festivals. A traditional harvest festival or a Messy Church session with a harvest theme could easily be expanded so that it becomes an extended programme of intergenerational activities in the home and at church, spread over several days. It could begin with families gathering fruit and vegetables from gardens and allotments (or supermarkets), then mucking in together at home (or at a massive cook-in at the church) to chop, mix, stir, boil and bake all manner of jams, chutneys, breads, pies and cakes for the feast after the harvest service. The feast could be combined with a barn dance, with invited guests. The following day, cakes and pies could be taken as gifts to neighbours, friends or work colleagues, with a word of explanation about wanting to share our celebration of all God's good gifts.

If only we were more intentional about building up our faith through all the different activities of our churches! This, it seems to me, is the key to whether an Old Testament-style discipleship programme of seasonal festivals plus faith at home actually works.

Key to the way that Messy Church is meant to work is the specific aim that people should not only have fun but also be encouraged to explore faith as they create things and chat about the Bible theme or story that links all of the crafts and the celebration. Those leading the crafts need training and practice in how to facilitate this sort of discussion in a gentle and unforced way.

To return to the harvest festival example, we could be more intentional about the faith-building element alongside the fun by printing take-home sheets giving suggestions for harvest games and crafts, Bible verses, prayer activities and questions to discuss. A wide variety of activities could be presented in a way that offers a range of opportunities over a period of a week or more for children and adults to celebrate and talk about God's creation and his wonderful provision for life. This would help to form disciples through memorable immersive learning experiences of worship and fellowship with the gathered church and at home.

Many aspects of our preparations for Christmas could be made more of in a similar way, and the week from Palm Sunday through to Easter Day offers numerous possibilities for processions, decorations, meaningful meals and memorable storytelling. Just add some intention and imagination, and stir.

For further thought and discussion:

✣ 'Belief and behaviour were nurtured with all generations together at both festival and family level.' From your experience, would you say this is possible or desirable today?

Chapter 4

Jesus and discipleship in the Gospels: kingdom community

Temple and synagogue

In the first two chapters of his Gospel, Luke describes Jesus' birth and upbringing in a context of faithful religious observance in the family home in Nazareth and at the temple in Jerusalem. Luke's account of Jesus visiting the temple when he was twelve years old provides us with a fascinating glimpse into the joyful, if somewhat chaotic, intergenerational holiday experience of travelling en masse from Galilee to Jerusalem for the Passover festival. Mary and Joseph are not perfect parents, and as a result they are an encouragement and example to all parents. They faithfully and successfully nurture the boy Jesus physically, mentally and spiritually in the context of the temple in Jerusalem, the synagogue in Nazareth and the family home. We can imagine the process of socialisation that was taking place over these years as they prayed for and with Jesus daily, talked about God's Law and the epic tale of God's dealing with his people, and retold the extraordinary story of Jesus' birth that Mary had treasured up in her heart.

The synagogue in Nazareth is where Jesus would have done his formal learning and heard and memorised the scriptures and set Jewish prayers. Of course, this is where Luke's Gospel depicts Jesus launching his ministry by reading from the prophet Isaiah, provoking both admiration and anger from all those who knew him as Joseph's son by his bold declaration, 'Today this scripture is fulfilled in your hearing' (Luke 4:14–30).

The name 'synagogue' comes from the Greek verb *synagō*, meaning 'to gather or bring together'. This local gathering for worship probably originated during the exilic period when it was no longer possible for Jews to worship in the temple in Jerusalem. Inevitably the development of the synagogue shifted the emphasis, for those who were too far from Jerusalem to travel there regularly, from the pattern of assembling together for sacrifice and ritual to meeting together for scripture reading, teaching and prayer.

In the Synoptic Gospels (Matthew, Mark and Luke) we regularly find Jesus in the local synagogue teaching, healing and driving out unclean spirits, and making friends and enemies as a result. His teaching is radically different from the customary formal style. Jesus teaches with authority. He does not back up his teaching in the usual way by referring to the received wisdom of previous rabbis, but simply states his view as the definitive ruling: 'You have heard it said... but *I* tell you...' (Matthew 5:21–22, 27–28, 31–34). He authenticates the authority of his words by commanding unclean spirits to be silent and depart (Luke 4:31–36). Like his cousin John the Baptist, Jesus is a radical and often preaches in the open air, urging people to 'Repent, for the kingdom of heaven has come near' (Matthew 4:17); in other words, to get ready for God's promised revolution.[17]

Followers of Jesus

Despite the different emphases of the authors or editors of the four Gospels, it is clear that Jesus was urging people to join a new community under his leadership in readiness for the messianic age that was now dawning.

Just as for Abraham, Jesus' call to discipleship in the Gospels begins with grace, with being chosen, but not because of one's own merit: 'You did not choose me, but I chose you and appointed you so that you might go and bear fruit—fruit that will last' (John 15:16). Tax collectors and sinners are welcomed and invited to spend time with Jesus at close quarters, and so they are challenged to believe in him and behave as he teaches. His sharing in meals with such unsuitable characters was a clear, powerful and controversial demonstration of the good news that God was graciously welcoming all sinners into his kingdom.

Again, as in the story of Abraham, those chosen by Jesus are called to leave their current way of life, radically readjusting their priorities. They must have sufficient trust and faith in Jesus to respond to, obey and follow him. Simon, Andrew, James and John abandon their fishing business, and Matthew the tax collector leaves his tax booth in response to Jesus' call to 'Follow me' (Matthew 4:18–22 and 9:9). In the New Testament the verb *akoloutheō*, meaning 'to follow behind', occurs almost exclusively in the Gospels. This is what an individual does as a disciple of Jesus in response to Jesus' personal call, for, unlike other rabbis, Jesus does not wait for people to ask to join him.

This decisive act of responding to Jesus' call, to his invitation to 'Take my yoke upon you and learn from me' (Matthew 11:28–30), seems to have been marked by baptism, not administered by Jesus himself, but by his disciples (see John 3:22–26; 4:1–2).[18] A committed and close relationship between teacher and pupil begins that brings both blessing and challenge.

Although Jesus is a gentle, humble teacher, whose yoke is easy, a readiness to take up one's cross, suffer and die for him is expected of all his followers (Matthew 16:24).

Apprentices of Jesus

The first disciples literally followed Jesus around, living with him and learning through imitation and experience, like apprentices learning skills from a master craftsman.

The New Testament word 'disciple' is *mathētēs* in Greek, meaning 'learner' or 'pupil'. It occurs 264 times, but only in the Gospels and Acts. It would have been familiar to Greek-speaking Jews, but it was given a totally new meaning in the Gospels to denote total lifelong attachment to someone as your master and teacher.

Jesus appointed the twelve, 'that they might be with him and that he might send them out to preach' (Mark 3:14). He required their assistance in his proclamation of God's kingdom, and quickly put his apprentices to work, even though their grasp of who Jesus was, what he meant by the phrase 'the kingdom of God' and the true nature of his mission was so inadequate that it clearly exasperated Jesus (for example, Matthew 16:5–11). Jesus regularly rebukes them as 'you of little faith' because of their feeble level of trust in him. They say and do the wrong things, reveal their selfish ambition for worldly power and glory, and have blazing rows with each other. One of them will betray their master, and the rest will desert him.

The Twelve fall short in all three aspects of belonging, believing and behaving. This is not surprising, because they have been thrust into leadership by Jesus while their faith is still in its infancy. Would a panel of selectors approve any of these characters for leadership roles in the church today, I wonder? Nevertheless, apprentices will never learn unless their master gives them real work to do, and allows them to make mistakes. This is, of course, what Jesus does as he sends the Twelve, and later the 72, out on mission.

This was a unique situation, however. Apart from flashes of God-given insight—such as when Peter blurts out, 'You are the Messiah,' in Matthew 16:16–17—a fuller understanding of the events the Twelve were caught up in was beyond them until after Jesus' resurrection and the intensive teaching he gave them during the 40 days before his ascension (see Acts 1:3). Our context as disciples is very different, because we have access to the whole story and the gift of the Holy Spirit, who teaches us and reminds us of the truth (John 14:26). Nevertheless, I wonder whether there is something we can learn from the way Jesus trains his apprentices, giving them challenges and responsibilities from an early stage in their apprenticeship.

Many non-churched people in Messy Church will have little knowledge or understanding of Jesus and the gospel, but they are keen to belong and play a part in Messy Church. In church, however, there is a tendency to give leadership responsibilities only to those who have been committed church members and have proved themselves to be 'sound' in belief and behaviour for many years, if not decades. There is a biblical precedent for this in Paul's instructions to Timothy regarding overseers and deacons (1 Timothy 3:1–13), and it is obviously important for key roles in the church. But if this policy is applied too broadly, it can mean, for instance, that young people are never elected to serve on church councils or given opportunities to lead initiatives. Is it any wonder they feel that church is not really for them?

I am amazed and ever grateful that the rural parish church where I was brought up had the faith and vision to encourage and allow me and three other teenage Christian friends to lead and preach at services occasionally, and to run the Sunday school, youth fellowship and an open youth group. They also passed a special rule reserving several places on the church council for 16–20-year-olds who were willing to be nominated. Regrettably, this sort of encouragement seems to be rare. Indeed, many adult Christians can go through their lives without ever having much responsibility in church. More importantly, many churchgoers never grasp the fact that they themselves are the frontline missionaries sent out by God to be salt and light in the places where they live and work. By not taking the apprenticeship model of learning seriously, we are missing some of the opportunities and risks that Jesus took to develop disciples by fully involving them in the challenges of his ministry and mission.

The dad who was brought along to Messy Church to help lead the craft is one example of the evangelistic effectiveness of a fast track into leadership. Another story comes from Le Fevre Uniting Church in Adelaide, Australia. When they started their Messy Church, the minister invited Deb to help out on the core team, although Deb's only previous link with church was through the toddler group and attending services occasionally for funerals, weddings and at Christmas. Only six months later, the whole team led an inspiring workshop on how to start a Messy Church, at the start of which Deb stood up and testified, 'I am now a Christian. Messy Church is my church, and I want to grow in my faith.' Eager to share what she had discovered, Deb had invited a teenager with learning difficulties, who was struggling to gain the necessary qualifications to leave school, to come and help lead a craft at Messy Church as a way of fulfilling her educational requirements. As the team met to pray before Messy Church, this teenager for the very first time experienced what it was like to be prayed for. Moved by this, she declared at the end of Messy Church that it had been 'the best day of my life'. To be caught up in God's mission can be extraordinarily affirming and life-changing, as we see from the joy of the 72 when they report back to Jesus in Luke 10:17.

One of the strengths of the Messy Church format is that it can help us to get away from the idea that church is run by the experts for all the rest. At Messy Church we can all become learners together. There are many opportunities to involve people of all ages and different levels of faith commitment in useful tasks and give them a taste of Christian service. If you invite a few prayerfully chosen non-churched people to join your planning team, then as you prepare the session together, discuss the theme, devise the crafts, plan the celebration and pray about it all, in effect you are involving them in a gentle form of group Bible study. In our own Messy Church in Cowplain it is obvious that involvement in the leadership team is helping teenagers and adults to grow as disciples, because being involved in mission stretches them and requires them to rely more on God as they discover and develop their gifts.

The Gospels show that lifelong discipleship often begins with a muddled and largely instinctive response to Jesus' call and character. It is possible to start your journey as a disciple long before you understand what you are taking on or have all your lifestyle issues sorted. Apprentices have to be allowed to make a mess of things in order to learn. They have to be given lots of fresh chances and plenty of encouragement for each small triumph and achievement. Apprenticeship is therefore an important and helpful way to reimagine discipleship as a process of acquiring Christian life skills through relationships where discipleship is modelled and practised under supervision. It is a helpful corrective to the church's tendency to emphasise formal learning, and it brings into sharper focus how we live out our faith in our daily lives.[19]

In Messy Church the opportunities for formal learning are limited, and our emphasis is certainly more on experiential learning. Jesus used both, as Bob Hopkins writes:

Jesus' model was one of making and growing disciples and leaders through coaching and apprenticeship. He also taught and trained on a larger scale, but his primary model was always around a small group community of learners whom he equipped for life and ministry. Jesus' method was also an expression of the Kingdom dynamic of multiplication. Training processes enable large numbers to be involved but are based on addition, with greater potential of short-term gain, whereas apprenticeship and coaching feeds into an ongoing relationship focused on fewer people but with long-term fruit that can be multiplied out to great longer-term potential.[20]

These are strong reasons why an apprenticeship model is one that Messy Church should develop more intentionally. However, there is one significant difference between the experiences of being an apprentice and being a disciple of Christ. Apprenticeship is usually only for a set time, and comes to an end when the student has acquired all the skills they need to branch out on their own, whereas those who become disciples of Christ will never fully qualify in this life. Apprenticeship to Jesus never ends. He is our master for ever.

The disciple as a child

Equally, if not more, challenging is a further strand of Jesus' teaching on discipleship in the Synoptic Gospels that the church has rarely (if ever) taken seriously—that is, Jesus' emphasis on the child as a model of true discipleship. The story is very familiar. Jesus is angry when he discovers that parents bringing children for him to bless are being sent away by his disciples. Children must be welcomed and allowed to come to him freely, he explains, because 'the kingdom of God belongs to such as these'. All disciples must be like children, because 'anyone who will not receive the kingdom of God like a little child will never enter it' (Mark 10:13–16).

What aspects of being a child did Jesus have in mind here? We cannot be sure, but, looking at the wider context in Mark 10, it is probably the child's total lack of status and importance. In first-century Jewish culture children were always at the back of the queue, valued largely for what they would grow up to be as adults. As children they had no status, possessions or power—the very things that adults tend to seek after and cling onto, but which Jesus saw as hindrances that prevent people from following him and entering the kingdom.

This is precisely the problem illustrated by the rich young man who runs up to Jesus just as he is about to move on after blessing the children (Mark 10:17–22). This young man comes rushing up to Jesus with the eagerness of a child, but after their conversation he goes away sad. His great wealth hinders him from receiving the kingdom of God like a child— with nothing but trust and a desire for blessing, living in the present moment with a healthy curiosity and an openness to new things.

For Jesus, these are precisely the qualities that all true disciples must cultivate. The Greek word for child in verses 13–15 is *paidion*, from the root *pou* or *pau*, meaning small. In verse 23 Jesus specifically calls the disciples 'children' as he turns to them and speaks about how hard it is for the rich to enter God's kingdom. Here Mark uses a different word, *tekna*, which also means 'child' but is derived from the verb *tiktein*, meaning 'to beget' or 'bear' a child. This word highlights the close bond between Jesus and his disciples, like that between a father and a son or a master and his pupils. It also strengthens the thematic link with Jesus' previous teaching on the need for disciples to receive the kingdom like a child.

These fundamental lessons on the disciple as a child in Mark's Gospel come just before Jesus' teaching on servant leadership and his final journey to Jerusalem, and surely ought to be part of our core curriculum in discipleship. I wonder whether, like the disciples, we hinder both children and ourselves from coming closer to Jesus by sending children away from our church services to be taught separately? Jesus calls a little child to come and stand in the middle of the disciples in Matthew 18:1–4 as a model of humility. We too need to bring children into the centre of church life, because to be 'great' disciples and enter the kingdom of heaven we must 'change and become like little children'.

Perhaps if Jesus were teaching this lesson today, he would bring into the centre other examples of those at the back of the queue, such as the unemployed, asylum seekers or the Dalit people of South Asia, whose name means 'suppressed', 'crushed' or 'broken to pieces'. The Dalit are treated as the lowest of the low and have to take on the most menial and filthy jobs.

True discipleship is learnt when we welcome the lowest person into our circle and become like them in total trust and dependence on Jesus. Messy Church seeks to welcome all into an intergenerational community where we can learn to be childlike in our relationship with Christ.

A disciple-making community

Vincent Donovan in *Christianity Rediscovered*, the classic account of his pioneering mission to the Masai people of North Tanzania, quotes Paul Tillich's description of the church as 'primarily a group of people who express a new reality by which they have been grasped'.[21] This description fits the community that Jesus gathers around himself in the Gospels.

Jesus calls into being an alternative community whose priority is God's kingdom and his way of life (Matthew 6:33). He does this through non-formal learning and relationships built with the inner circle of Peter, James and John, the Twelve, and later the 72, and through more formal teaching to the wider group of disciples (for example, in the Sermon on the Mount).

The disciples' loyalty is to Jesus even when they face persecution (Matthew 5:11). Their behaviour is wisely and firmly built on Jesus' example and teaching (Matthew 7:24–27). Like God's people in the Old Testament, this alternative community has been called for mission, to be salt and light, to bring God's promised blessing to the world (Matthew 5:13–16). Matthew's Gospel ends with the great commission of the risen Lord in chapter 28:16–20 to 'go and make disciples of all nations', echoing the commissioning of Abraham in Genesis 12.[22] The promise to Abraham of being a blessing to all the nations will be fulfilled as the community of the risen Christ tells the gospel story, calls people to respond in faith with baptism and forms them into disciples who live the Jesus way.

In the Gospels, discipleship is learnt alongside others in a community, with Christ as the teacher to obey and the model to imitate. Jesus models humble service, love and sacrifice. He teaches his disciples to pray to God as 'Our Father' with faith and brevity, encouraging them to ask for the Holy Spirit. There were some secret disciples, like Joseph of Arimathea and Nicodemus (John 19:38–39), who were privileged to receive private one-to-one teaching from Jesus, but usually the disciples are seen learning together. Mary sat at Jesus' feet and listened, but Martha should have chosen to leave the kitchen and sit there too (Luke 10:38–41).

There are only three spiritual disciplines that Jesus says his disciples must do secretly and not in front of others. These are giving to the needy, prayer and fasting (Matthew 6:1–18). Disciples need to learn to take individual responsibility for these so that they can enjoy and maintain a personal relationship with their heavenly Father and avoid the empty hypocrisy of seeking to impress others with their piety.[23] Nevertheless, these disciplines are developed by individuals who are 'children' or pupils together, members of an alternative, kingdom-focused, disciple-making community with Jesus as master and model.

How effectively are we modelling discipleship in community so that people can learn from it? What can we hope to achieve in just one hour per week (perhaps supplemented with a house group evening for the keenest), or 2½ hours per month in Messy Church? There is clearly a need to give more time, thought, planning and training for this task in Messy Church so that we can make the most of the time we have together. We should aspire to the ideal expressed by one Messy Church leader that, 'From the moment they walk in the door, everything we do is about making disciples.'

Discipleship as love in action

In contrast to the three Synoptic Gospels, John's Gospel gives us a differently nuanced answer to the question, 'What is a disciple?' John moves us on from the literal meaning of *akoloutheō* as following behind Jesus. 'I am the light of the world,' says Jesus. 'Whoever follows me will never walk in darkness, but will have the light of life' (John 8:12). He assures the Twelve, 'I am the way and the truth and the life. No one comes to the Father except through me' (John 14:6).

In John's Gospel, being a disciple of Jesus is no longer about having sufficient faith to follow him and be his apprentice. Instead, it is more specifically about believing that this man is the way to God, salvation and life. This can be seen in John's statement of purpose:

> *Jesus performed many other signs in the presence of his disciples, which are not recorded in this book. But these are written that you may believe that Jesus is the Messiah, the Son of God, and that by believing you may have life in his name.*

JOHN 20:30–31

John, moreover, records Jesus' words at the Last Supper that the single universally recognisable mark of Christian discipleship is Christ-like love for one another. 'By this everyone will know that you are my disciples, if you love one another' (John 13:34–35).

Laying down your life, taking up your cross, is now something done for others in imitation of Jesus. Here we see even more clearly than in the Synoptic Gospels that Christian discipleship is a communal activity. You simply cannot be recognised as a disciple on your own. For non-believing people to say, 'Those are disciples of Jesus,' there needs to be a community that knows the story of Jesus' service and sacrifice, believes Jesus is the way to life, and models Jesus' love. 'As the Father has sent me, I am sending you' (John 20:21).

Gospel pointers for disciple-making in Messy Church

What, then, can we learn for disciple-making in Messy Church from the way that Jesus made disciples?

1. **We must begin by welcoming and accepting all people** just as they are, with all their faults and baggage, as a sign of God's grace, as Jesus welcomed and ate with tax collectors and sinners. Let them be with us and be blessed and have a taste of belonging to God's kingdom community.
2. **We need to recognise that disciples are made in a community** where the risen Christ is our leader and model. Are we intentionally operating in our Messy Church community in such a way that disciple-making can happen?
3. **Disciple-making requires more intentional, non-formal, apprenticeship-style experiential learning** than we are accustomed to in our churches, with more mentoring and coaching, learning through experience and being sent out on mission.
4. **There are times when individuals or smaller groups need to be drawn aside from the larger group for more formal training and learning**, just as Jesus spent time with his inner circle of Peter, James and John and with the Twelve.
5. **Good relationships are vital**, and require much time and commitment to develop. There must be patience when

progress is slow, forgiveness for failures and encouragement for progress, even the smallest steps.

6. **Those who are leaders must be prepared to give of themselves to people** and to have their lives on show as humble, imperfect models of discipleship. Jesus led his disciples in an intensive three-year immersive learning experience.

7. **As an intergenerational community we must welcome and bless the lowest and the least**, and seek to learn together what it means to have a childlike relationship with the Father.

8. **We need to focus on learning very practically how to love and serve one another** as the universally recognised sign that we are Christ's disciples.

For further thought and discussion:

✣ 'Church is meant to be an alternative kingdom-focused community.' To what extent do you think this is true of your church?

✣ How important is Jesus' teaching on the disciple as a child?

Chapter 5

Disciples in Acts

Followers of the Way

Although following Jesus is what disciples do in the Gospels, this is surprisingly not how disciples are described in the rest of the New Testament. The verb *akolouthe̅o* appears only three times in Acts. Although still frequently described as 'disciples', they are now also called 'saints', 'brothers' and 'believers', but not 'followers of Jesus Christ'. The terminology has changed, and in those early days of the church, disciples were commonly known as followers of the Way or those who 'belonged to the Way' (Acts 9:2). Paul describes himself as 'a follower of the Way' in Acts 24, insisting that this is not a sect but a proper development of Jewish faith.

What was 'the Way' shorthand for? There are hints in phrases such as 'the way of the Lord' and 'the way of God' (Acts 18:25–26), which show the influence of Jesus' declaration that he is 'the way' to the Father (John 14:6).[24] In Philippi, the fortune-telling slave girl who follows Paul and his companions shouts out, 'These men are… telling you the way to be saved' (Acts 16:17). There has been a shift away from the rabbinic language of following a master or teacher used in the Gospels. Instead, the believers' commitment to the risen and ascended Christ is seen as like being on a trail that Christ has blazed for us. We follow his way through life, which leads us to God's salvation.

Acts also records that Antioch is where the disciples are first nicknamed 'Christians' by the locals (Acts 11:26). This is the type of name that was often given to a group of supporters of a political leader, for example, the Herodians who supported Herod the Great. It suggests that the disciples were seen by ordinary people in Antioch as a group with a different world view, distinctive beliefs, values, loyalties and ways of behaving that were entered into by those who believed Jesus to be 'both Lord and Messiah'.

This last phrase is the punchline of Peter's sermon on the Day of Pentecost in Acts 2:36, and Paul presents the same idea in a different way to a pagan audience in Athens in Acts 17:22–31. Becoming a Christian by accepting Jesus as Lord is a political act. You are joining an alternative community whose allegiance is to Christ as the coming Judge and true King of all.

Disciple-making in Acts

How were disciples made during this early period of the church following the pouring-out of the Holy Spirit on the Day of Pentecost? Although the main concern of Luke, the author of Acts, is to tell the story of the fulfilment of Jesus' words in Acts 1:8—how the Spirit-empowered witness of the apostles went out from Jerusalem to the ends of the earth—he does also provide us with some insights into how new followers were guided on 'the Way'.

As the apostles and their assistants travelled to each new centre of population, the good news of Jesus crucified, risen and reigning was proclaimed first to Jews and then to Gentiles. The non-Jewish people they encountered included proselytes (Gentile converts to Judaism), those who were sympathetic to the Jewish faith but not converts, and those who were believers in the pagan gods. All were called in the same way to repent, believe and be baptised.

Baptism of new believers took place immediately after an initial response of repentance and faith and without more than brief preparation. There are nine instances in Acts of converts being baptised without delay. These are the 3,000 converted at Pentecost (Acts 2:38, 41); the Samaritans (Acts 8:12); the Ethiopian eunuch (Acts 8:37–38); the apostle Paul (after three days of blindness, Acts 9:18; 22:16); the first Gentile converts (Acts 10:47–48); Lydia (Acts 16:14–15); the Philippian jailer and his household (Acts 16:31–33); the Corinthians (Acts 18:8); and the twelve disciples of John the Baptist (Acts 19:3–5). Baptism marked and sealed the individual's conversion, as they received God's forgiveness and the gift of the Spirit (Acts 2:38). Teaching and training in the way of the Lord followed afterwards within the newly formed community. We see this in Acts 2:42–47, where the believers spend much time together worshipping, learning from the apostles, developing in generosity and caring for one another. Similarly, in Acts 10, following the baptism of Cornelius and his Gentile household, Peter is asked to stay for a few days, presumably to give them further instruction.

When Paul and Silas set off on their first missionary journey, opposition to their message means that they have to leave Pisidian Antioch after only eight days (Acts 13:13–51). On their return journey, however, they are able to revisit the new believers, 'strengthening the disciples and encouraging them to remain true to the faith', and appointing elders in each church

(Acts 14:21–23). These churches were presumably quite small groups meeting in homes.

Paul seems to prefer, when he can, to stay in a place for some time 'strengthening and encouraging' the believers after their baptism. Sometimes he is forced to move on quickly, and has to leave his colleagues in charge and make a return visit later, as in Berea (Acts 17:10–15).

There are a few episodes in Acts where there is apparently little or no opportunity for post-baptismal instruction of new disciples. An obvious one is the account of the conversion and baptism of the Ethiopian court treasurer on the Gaza road. Philip has barely finished baptising this man before the Spirit whisks Philip away (Acts 8:26–40), making him the patron saint of evangelists who buzz in to preach, then buzz off, leaving others to do the follow-up! One hopes that the Spirit sent someone else along to help this new believer take his first steps on the Way.

Another instance is the conversion of the jailer in Philippi (Acts 16:16–40). Paul and Silas have been stripped, beaten and flung into jail. Bloody but unbowed, they are leading a midnight praise and prayer meeting when a violent earthquake shakes the prison and all the doors fly open. This wakes the jailer, who assumes that the prisoners have escaped and prepares to kill himself before his superiors find out and sentence him to a worse fate. Paul calls out to him to stop, because they are all still present and correct. The jailer falls before Paul, crying, 'What must I do to be saved?' Paul and Silas explain the gospel to him and his family, and the jailer and his household are baptised straight away, even though it is the small hours of the morning. They then share a celebratory meal, and, by daybreak, Paul and Silas are protesting to the magistrates about their illegal imprisonment and demanding to be formally escorted out of the prison. Amid the drama of this night there is insufficient time for even the briefest discipleship course. Presumably this task was left to the church that met at Lydia's house, where Paul had already spent some time doing the usual encouraging and strengthening (Acts 16:14–15, 40).

What form did Paul's 'encouraging and strengthening' take? Acts 20 provides some clues, where we see Paul spending a week at Troas. At the gathering for the breaking of bread on Paul's final evening with them, Paul shows his nocturnal predilection again as he preaches on until past midnight (*dialegomai*, the Greek verb used here, means to talk, argue, reason, discuss, instruct). A young man called Eutychus nods off, and falls from the third-floor window to his death. Paul rushes down and raises the young man to life. Then, after breaking bread and eating, Paul continues to instruct what must have been a weary but astonished congregation until his departure at daybreak (Acts 20:7–12).

It would seem that Paul was keen to make the most of the time he had on these visits to provide formal teaching about Christian belief and to exhort the believers to live by it. This was an urgent priority for Paul while he was with them, because it was something that local elders might not have been able to do, simply because they were comparatively new Christians and lacking in knowledge and experience.

Later in the same chapter, as Paul bids farewell to the Ephesian elders (Acts 20:13–38), he reminds them how he preached and taught formally in public and less formally from house to house, proclaiming 'the whole will of God'. His parting advice to the elders is to keep watch over themselves and their flock, because false teachers will come like savage wolves to attack them. As he commits them to God's grace, he reminds them of his own example of hard work and generosity and the words of the Lord Jesus himself: 'It is more blessed to give than to receive.'

Paul's greatest concern here is that young disciples should be protected from false teaching, and that church leaders should model for them the compassion, generosity and sacrifice of Christ. In other words, what needs to be encouraged, strengthened and moreover modelled by the leaders is both right belief and right behaviour—life lived in accordance with the teaching and example of Jesus.

To summarise our findings: in Acts the gospel is preached by the apostles as they travel from place to place. Those who respond with repentance and faith are baptised at once, and then instructed by the apostle or one of his colleagues. Churches are formed, meeting in homes under the leadership of elders appointed by the apostle or one of his colleagues. It is in these small groups that ongoing Christian formation takes place through formal instruction (supplemented by return visits by the apostle or his colleagues) and non-formal modelling and socialisation within the church community.

Some of the converts, perhaps the majority to begin with, were from a Jewish background, or were proselytes or God-fearing Gentiles, like Cornelius and Lydia. They would have had some grounding in the Old Testament and Jewish prayers. Others were from a pagan background and would have needed to be taught everything from scratch, such as the Philippian jailer and his household (which probably included children). Luke says in Acts 16:34 that the jailer 'had come to believe in God—he and his whole household', which suggests that his background was that of a believer in the pagan gods rather than the one true God.

Making disciples in the early church was therefore heavily dependent on the effectiveness of these extremely young local churches and their inexperienced leaders to apply the formal apostolic teaching to a very mixed flock. Despite this, once Paul had established a church in a place and spent some time there, he considered his work there complete (see Romans 15:23). Paul saw the ongoing evangelism and disciple-making in these places as being the task of the local church. It probably took different forms, depending on the context and what background the converts were from. Shaped by mission, guided by the Spirit, a simple and informal network of churches emerged that enabled rapid development and growth, even at a time when long-distance travel was perilous and communication was difficult.

What can we learn from all this? As Messy Church has spread, across the UK and internationally, BRF's Messy Church Team, assisted by the Regional and International Coordinators (mostly volunteers), have found themselves in a quasi-apostolic role, travelling far and wide to encourage the development of local Messy Churches that share the vision and DNA of the movement. Every Messy Church is locally led and effectively free to develop its own contextualised way of being a disciple-making community, while still having the support of the Messy Church network. Like the developing church described in Acts, this is a 'light touch', hands-off structure shaped by and for mission and growth. Care needs to be taken that it continues to be a movement and avoids the tendency to become a more centralised organisation.

As in Acts, young Messy Churches, and in particular their leaders, require a great deal of support, strengthening and encouragement from the BRF team and their colleagues if they are to be equipped to help people on their journey into faith and discipleship. It will be important for Messy Churches to feel that they are really loved, cared for and prayed for by the team and that each church has a strong bond with one or more members of the team. Team members will need to make visits to Messy Churches and provide support in the form of consultation, training, resources and even epistles (letters)—or, more likely, emails, blogs and tweets.

Interestingly, the only mention Luke makes of a letter being sent for the instruction of the churches is the epistle from the Jerusalem Council regarding Gentile believers in Acts 15, but there were, of course, many other letters, to which we now turn.

For further thought and discussion:

✤ What do you think were the particular strengths and weaknesses of the early church? How do they compare and contrast with the strengths and weaknesses of today's church?
✤ What sort of 'encouraging and strengthening' do you think Messy Church leaders need so that they can disciple their very mixed flock?

Chapter 6

Disciple-making in the Epistles and Revelation

Sending letters was one of the main ways in which Paul and others strengthened belief and encouraged Christian behaviour across a far-flung and growing network of churches.

Though Paul preferred to make personal visits to churches if he could, when he was prevented by persecution or other circumstances, he often sent a colleague with a letter to be read out in the assembly addressing the particular issues of belief and behaviour in that church. Some of these epistles were also intended for wider circulation among the churches (see Colossians 4:16).

The book of Revelation serves a similar purpose, although the letters in this book are from Christ himself to a group of seven specific churches in Asia. As such they are placed within the context of an apocalyptic revelation of Christ as Lord, which is intended to encourage believers not to lose hope or give up the Christian way.

Although the epistles and Revelation were clearly motivated by a concern to encourage ongoing discipleship, the actual word 'disciple' does not appear in the New Testament after the book of Acts. Believers are instead referred to as 'the saints' (i.e. holy ones), 'brothers', 'children of God', those 'who are in Christ Jesus' and 'servants of God'. That the term 'disciple' is never used in addressing these young believers may seem odd to us. It reflects a further shift of emphasis from individuals as disciples of Christ to a more collective way of understanding membership of the church, which has more in common with the Old Testament concept of God's holy people and nation (1 Peter 2:9). The belief and behaviour of this alternative community, those 'in Christ' who are 'the body of Christ', is meant to demonstrate to the world God's steadfast love through Christ. This is similar to Jesus' teaching about being a community of love, being salt in the world and letting your light shine (John 13:34–35; Matthew 5:13–16).

The epistles address particular issues of faith and practice that affect a church's unity and holiness—community discipleship, in effect. Paul's method in his letters is to tackle local problems by calling attention to particular aspects of the gospel and doctrine, then urging his hearers to make the appropriate behavioural response to the grace of God: right belief leading to right behaviour. A good example of this is in 1 Corinthians, where Paul deals with divisions in the church by expounding the power and wisdom of the cross and the unity in diversity of the body of Christ.

Saints need to become as a community what they already are by grace: a holy people, set apart as God's own. Believers become more and more like Christ by cooperating with the transforming work of the Spirit (2 Corinthians 3:18; Romans 12:2). Every member should play his or her part in the life of the church 'so that the body of Christ may be built up until we all reach unity in the faith and in the knowledge of the Son of God and become mature, attaining to the whole measure of the fullness of Christ' (Ephesians 4:12–13). Brothers and sisters are to be Christ to each other and imitate Christ as they see his life modelled in the lives of Paul and other leaders (1 Corinthians 11:1; Hebrews 13:7). Paul tells the Galatians that he feels 'the pains of childbirth until Christ is formed in you' (Galatians 4:19).

In 1 Thessalonians 1:9–10 Paul gives a three-point description of the church in Thessalonica as those who have turned from idols to serve the living and true God and to wait for his Son from heaven. In other words, there is a break with the past, a changed life in the present and a future hope. He encourages them to 'live lives worthy of God' (1 Thessalonians 2:12). Having previously instructed them 'how to live in order to please God', he urges them to make the effort to do so 'more and more' (1 Thessalonians 4:1).

The various writers of the epistles are in agreement that saints must act intentionally to change their behaviour: 'Clothe yourselves with the Lord Jesus Christ, and do not think about how to gratify the desires of the flesh' (Romans 13:14). They are urged to 'put to death' things that belong to the sinful nature and 'put on the new self, which is being renewed in knowledge in the image of its Creator' (Colossians 3:10; cf. Ephesians 4:23). The writer to the Hebrews tells believers to fix their eyes on Jesus as a model for the faithful endurance of a true son of the Father (Hebrews 12:2–11). John repeatedly stresses that Christ-like love in action must be evident in the church community (1 John 3:11–18).

The local church is seen as a holy priesthood, a temple of living stones declaring the glory of God (1 Peter 2:4–10). It is a colony of the coming King of Kings (Philippians 3:20). It is a community in which, as the Holy Spirit transforms minds and behaviour, all the members are growing to maturity in Christ.

The epistles and Revelation assume that development and growth in discipleship happens in the church community through non-formal learning and a process of socialisation. It is not simply about an individual's deepening faith and developing spirituality, which is how we often tend to think about spiritual growth. It is about people of all ages and backgrounds growing together into maturity within the body of Christ. This process of 'resocialisation' or 'the transformation of their beliefs, their sense of belonging and their patterns of behaviour,'[25] takes place as the believers meet together regularly in homes for prayer, worship and mutual encouragement.

As yet there are no formal basics groups or discipleship courses, no groups specifically for men, women, children or teenagers. Paul and the other leaders clearly spend much time giving more formal instruction to the whole church and individuals, but it is in community that the saints learn and practise how to love one another and confess their failings to each other. Gathered together, they receive practical guidance and support for living a holy life day by day in their relationships at home with their parents, husbands, wives and children, and at work, whether they are a master or a slave.

This looks something like Bob Hopkins' definition of church as 'a Jesus community of discipleship making disciples'. Hopkins goes on to argue that 'the degradation of Christendom is due to the loss of this function, much more effectively performed over the generations by extended Christian family and Christian schools than by what we called church—a Sunday event in a religious building.'[26]

When we gather together as the local church, it is usually for worship rather than practical training in Christian living. We have developed further meetings, groups and courses in an attempt to make up for this, but often less than half of our church members opt into these extras. As a result many churchgoers say their faith seems irrelevant and disconnected from daily life, and they feel ill-equipped to make these connections themselves. Our church community life is lacking, and our disciple-making is weak as a result.[27]

George Lings suggests that the church can learn valuable lessons about community from the monastic tradition, particularly from observing the way monasteries and Christian communities have tended to organise their buildings. Lings identifies seven sacred spaces that have been essential to this form of Christian community: cell, chapel, chapter, cloister, garden, refectory and scriptorium.[28]

For centuries the church has tended to give more time, energy and importance to Sunday services than to any other activity, but in the monastic community this is 'chapel', just one of the seven important spaces in which the Christian community functions. Growing and sustaining a Christian community requires much more than simply meeting regularly for worship. Yet most people's idea of a church building is a chapel and nothing more, a place set aside for worship, rather than a building that offers different spaces for other important community activities. For example, there could be a 'refectory' for offering hospitality and eating together ('vital to the informal socialisation of new members'[29]) or a 'cloister' where people can meet informally. Serving coffee at the back or in the church hall after services is a token recognition that we do need other sacred spaces to sustain Christian community.

A Messy Church session offers different 'spaces' for greeting, meeting, creating, celebrating and eating together, although it often requires considerable creativity and furniture-shifting to modify and use the spaces we have in our church buildings.

The 'chapel' element in Messy Church, the celebration, is the shortest part of the session, usually about 15 minutes. This might be seen as a 'teaching' slot, an opportunity to tell a Bible story and get across a lesson. I view it somewhat differently, as a drawing together of everything that has been going on—the conversations, the crafts, the 'God moments' when people saw something of the kingdom, and all the different forms of learning that have been happening, formal, non-formal and socialisation, during the previous hour. We celebrate what we have made and reinforce the links with the Bible theme or story. We invite people to respond to God in praise and prayer, to express the things they have been thinking and feeling. It is interactive and exploratory rather than didactic, and we often ask wondering questions, similar to those used in the reflective storytelling of Godly Play (a creative approach to Christian nurture developed in the USA by Dr Jerome Berryman using reflective storytelling, wondering questions and open-ended response time).

At St Wilfrid's we have introduced a new element into our celebration called 'A History of Our Faith in 100 Objects'. Announced by a fanfare, a different person each month is given two minutes to show and tell us about an object that has a link with their faith journey. For Bob it was a windsurfing board, recalling how he became a Christian after hearing the gospel from a friend on a windsurfing holiday. For Lesley it was a sticky note, because she thought nobody read the Bible until she found that her friend's Bible was full of sticky notes marking all the exciting bits through which God had spoken to her friend. This made Lesley curious to start reading the Bible for herself. 'A History of Our Faith in 100 Objects' is a short, simple way to give a glimpse of God at work in people's lives. It builds up those speaking about their chosen object and gives them more confidence to talk about their faith. It intrigues the hearers and provokes questions over the meal table.

The meal that follows the celebration is an essential part of the programme where socialisation is happening. Christian faith and values can be modelled, observed and discussed around the tables. It is also important community-building time, as we sing a special song for all those with a birthday during the month: 'A happy birthday to you… Every day of the year may you feel Jesus near.'

It has been suggested that more use could be made of the meal time to explore discipleship, perhaps forming regular groups meeting around a table with a designated leader to facilitate discussion. To me this seems too formal and threatening for our context, as well as difficult to organise, but placing a card on each table with an optional question for discussion linked to the day's theme can easily be done. 'Table Talk' discussion-starter cards for use at Messy Church or at home have been devised.[30]

Claire Dalpra notes from her research into fresh expressions of church that 'one congregational worship gathering struggles to adequately respond to the diversity of not-yet Christians, new Christians and existing Christians'. Consequently, she says, lay-led fresh expressions of church often find they need to develop midweek sub-gatherings (larger than house groups) with a discipleship element.[31] In our experience, families have been reluctant to take on something extra that might be too 'heavy' and religious. One Messy Church in Australia has tried to resolve this by offering an optional discussion group during part of the craft time. Similarly, at St Wilfrid's we have occasionally invited families who have expressed an interest in finding out about baptism to spend part of the craft time doing this as a group. We also provide a number of quiet, reflective prayer activities in the main worship area while the crafts are going on in the adjoining hall, and we find that adults and children do come through to make use of these. There is certainly scope for offering a wider variety of activities and 'spaces' during the craft time.

Many Messy Churches have established additional meetings during the month. These range from a simple 'Messy Meet-up' after school, a purely social gathering without the pressure to provide a full programme of activities, to groups using formal introductory courses such as Alpha and Start.

'Deeper Mess' at St Philips Church, Dronfield, offered Advent experiences of alternative worship and an intergenerational cell group. In Cowplain we have had a monthly 'Messy Tea' on a Sunday afternoon, attended mainly, but not exclusively, by the team. Here large quantities of cake are eaten while we discuss an aspect of Messy Church and how we could be more effective. We are also experimenting with a Sunday lunch format. Others have tried one-off extras such as a Messy Church 'Footsteps of Jesus' day, making costumes and props and going round the village telling the story, and a 'Tea Shop' evening on 'What is church for?'

Clearly, though, many of the non-churched families who attend Messy Church are not at a stage where they see the need to join another group or a course, and would not feel comfortable in doing so. They lead busy lives, and are reluctant to commit themselves to coming more than once a month, just like many 'regular' Sunday churchgoers. So for most people the disciple-making agenda cannot be shifted entirely to a second meeting. It has to be addressed in the main meeting, not only for this pragmatic reason, but because the New Testament says growth to maturity in Christ happens as we all play our part together in the body of Christ. Evangelism and disciple-making belong together like a horse and cart, and should not be separated. As disciples share and live the gospel, they grow in faith themselves, and new disciples are made, who imitate them and learn from them how to live and share the good news with others—disciples making disciples in community.

Messy Church, with its informal approach and variety of community spaces and experiences within the session, can potentially make vital connections between belief and behaviour, faith and everyday life. With training, support and resourcing, Messy Churches can be more intentional about using the whole session to model, encourage and practise Christian living.

Some Messy Churches decide, for what may seem like good practical reasons, to leave out one or more of the key elements. Often it is the meal that goes. Perhaps serving a full meal is difficult in their premises or is felt to involve too much work or expense, but if they are serious about making disciples, they should think twice about this. Messy Church aims to be much more than a craft club for children; it can be an alternative disciple-making community where people are learning together to love God and one another in imitation of Jesus. Together we can learn to forgive and be a blessing to others. Together, as we all use our gifts, we can encourage one another in working out how to live by these values in our families and with our neighbours, at school and at work.

For further thought and discussion:

✢ Which of the seven sacred spaces does your church provide? Which are lacking, and what could you do about it?

✢ 'The church is a disciple-making community.' How wide is the gap between your experience of church and this ideal? What are the first steps to take towards this?

Chapter 7

A community discipleship curriculum

What might a curriculum for a disciple-making community look like?

In August 2011 I attended an in-service training event entitled 'Messy Ministry in Context', hosted by the Uniting Church in Sydney, Australia, for pastors and those working with youth, children and families. Alongside sessions on Messy Church and Godly Play, Duncan Macleod, Presbytery Minister with the Canberra Region Presbytery, led two sessions on setting ministry in context. He used material developed for the Queensland Synod of the Uniting Church of Australia as part of the *Mission Stories* study programme.[32] It was refreshing to hear Macleod emphasise the fact that faith is not something acquired by and grown in individual Christians, but that it should be in the local church as a community that we are working out together how to live out the gospel in the wider world and grow as disciples.

Macleod went on to present for discussion a list of twelve aspects of the gospel that a church needs to know and show, grasp and share with the world. These twelve gospel values and the type of community they should lead to are:

Gospel of Forgiveness: New beginnings
  Forgiven and Forgiving Community

Gospel of Welcome, Belonging, Adoption, New Family
  Welcomed and Welcoming Community

Gospel of Calling and Service: building, sowing, sewing, washing…
  Served and Serving in Community

Gospel of Servant Leadership: socially responsible, proactive, future-focused
  Led and Leading Community

Gospel of Reconciliation: removing walls of prejudice, fear and enmity
  Reconciled and Reconciling Community

Gospel of Solidarity in Suffering
  Supported and Supporting Those Who Suffer in Community

Gospel of Healing: Wholeness for body, soul, mind, community
  Healed and Healing Community

Gospel of Courage: Capacity to stand for justice, against injustice
  Empowered, Encouraged and Empowering Community

Gospel of Liberation: Freedom and release
  Liberated and Liberating Community

Gospel of Transformation: Change in priorities for people, communities, societies, systems
  Transformed and Transforming Community

Gospel of Creation: God's pleasure in God's handiwork
  Created and Creating/Nurturing Community

Gospel of Insight: knowledge, wisdom, truth that guides and opens
  Learning and Wisdom-Sharing Community.[33]

For me this was like the moment when a light bulb comes on above a cartoon character's head. Here was a fresh vision and curriculum for making disciples in an all-age community such as Messy Church. For example, because the good news of Jesus is about forgiveness and new beginnings, so the local community of disciples needs to be learning and growing together in forgiveness. This means growing to know in their hearts that they are forgiven by God, and working out in practice how to become a more forgiving community—forgiving one another and forgiving others outside the community of faith.

While these twelve areas might not cover everything a disciple-making community needs to be (I would be keen to add a 'Blessed and Blessing Community' dealing with aspects of generosity and giving), they provide a stimulating outworking of the Five Marks of Mission[34] and are enough to keep any church busy. They are challenging, demanding far more than the acquisition of knowledge through formal learning, and they force us to face up to real issues of learning to live together and love one another. All twelve areas relate to very practical aspects of everyday life that affect us all, and that people of all ages could explore and engage with together at church and at home in families. There are plans to develop this scheme into a book, DVD and study course, and it would be good if all-age material could be included here.

It is refreshing to see church life described in this dynamic language. It provides an alternative way of looking at the maturity of a church community and a checklist for assessing strengths and weaknesses. I can easily see areas in which Messy Church is working well and others where we could work more intentionally on our informal disciple-making under these headings. For instance, Messy Church is good at being a welcoming community, but are we also helping individuals to be more welcoming and accepting in their daily lives? What are we doing in our Messy Church about solidarity with those who suffer, or transforming the wider community?

To be a 'served and serving' community is already part of Messy Church's DNA. Many children and adults who come to Messy Church have their first taste of the gospel when a total stranger from the catering team serves them a hot meal. When team members, dads, mums and children all muck in to help clear away the tables and sweep the floor at the end, we are learning together to serve others. When Messy Church collects small change to sponsor the building of a toilet in Burundi, we are becoming an empowered and empowering community, modelling a concern for justice and wider world issues.[35] When we take creation as our theme, the crafts and celebration can help us to engage with what it means for us to be a creative and nurturing community and to explore practical ways in which we can show care for God's creation in our daily lives.

The process of Christian formation in community that Macleod's gospel values require would bring us much closer to the pattern we have seen in the New Testament, in the book of Acts and the epistles, where disciple-making took place without sophisticated and expensive programmes or formal structures. Obviously in the early church there were often problems, difficulties, setbacks and disappointments due to wrong beliefs and bad behaviour. Disciple-making will no doubt be just as messy in our very different contexts today. Nevertheless we should persevere, like the apostle Paul, who always gave thanks for the saints, assuring them of his love and ceaseless prayers, and affirming them as his 'glory and joy' (1 Thessalonians 2:20).

For further thought and discussion:

✛ What do you think are the main ways in which our church community should be different from our contemporary culture?

✛ Which of the twelve gospel themes outlined by Macleod do you feel is the greatest challenge to you and your church community?

✛ What would need to happen for your church to become a community that lives out all twelve of Macleod's gospel values? What are the first steps?

Chapter 8

An alternative—catechesis then and now

The catchphrase 'We've always done it this way' may often be heard in church circles, but it is certainly not true of Christian formation down the centuries. In the first half of the second century a radical change took place in the way that Christian disciples were made.

In the first-century church, discipleship began with a response to the good news of Jesus. Repentance and faith led to baptism and then a lifelong process of non-formal Christian formation in the church community. However, by the second half of the second century in Rome we find Justin (a former student of Greek philosophy who became one of the great teachers and defenders of the Christian faith) preparing candidates for baptism with a three-year formal programme of catechesis, covering both doctrine and behaviour.[36]

How did such a major change come about? Although evidence from this period is limited, the change seems to have been in response to the fact that it was illegal and potentially dangerous to be a Christian. You had to be careful who you talked to about your faith and circumspect about revealing who the members of the local church were. This led to a more cautious approach to evangelism. In this context there could be no such thing as public worship or seeker-sensitive services; unless you were baptised, you were not allowed to attend. Seekers or enquirers who were found to have a genuine interest in the faith were catechised and expected to show a definite change in their behaviour before they could be baptised and join the worshipping community. So both believing and behaving were now required before baptism and belonging. The only Christians the candidates would meet before baptism would be their catechist and a Christian sponsor or mentor who helped to monitor their progress and prayed and fasted with them.

Before his conversion, Justin had been impressed by the way Christians lived out their faith and endured persecution. Similarly in the third century, Cyprian, a wealthy and gifted man from Carthage, found his high-flying aristocratic lifestyle 'darkness and gloomy night' compared to the freedom he experienced when a Christian friend took him to meet members of the local church. Cyprian sold his estates and enrolled as a catechumen (someone preparing for baptism). He went through a profound inner struggle because he found it hard to behave and live as the Christians taught. In both Justin's and Cyprian's accounts of their conversion there is clear evidence of the profound influence the countercultural lifestyle of the believing community had upon them. What they had heard about this community and experienced through meeting Christians was powerfully attractive.

Catechesis, with its insistence on commitment to a lengthy process, was undoubtedly a much more rigorous method for making disciples who would take their place in an alternative kingdom community and be committed to it. For this reason, Church historian Alan Kreider, who laments our failure to make disciples today, strongly recommends catechesis as the answer. This method has continued to be used in the Roman Catholic Church, and other traditions have adopted and adapted it in various ways. As a formal process, it would appear to be at the opposite end of the spectrum from the informality of Messy Church, but I think there are a number of insights that we should take on board.

1. **The importance of context.** The New Testament and church history show us that disciple-making has taken different forms in different times and places. In making disciples today, the Church needs to draw on the wisdom and experience of the past. However, we should avoid making the assumption that there is a single God-given method for guaranteed success. As we build relationships with non-churched people and accompany them on their journey towards faith, we will need to rediscover and devise appropriate ways of making disciples in different contexts.

   It is in this sense that Messy Church will need to reinvent discipleship, as Bishop Paul Butler said, but this need not involve reinventing the wheel every time. Perhaps, to stretch the analogy, we are redesigning the wheel for use in a different terrain. In other words, the heart of what a disciple is remains the same today as it was for the apostle Paul, but how disciples are made and how they learn to live out their faith will vary with context.

2. **The emphasis in catechesis on behaviour and knowledge, both the will and the mind, is very important.** Teaching in the form of sermons and courses has tended to place too much emphasis on our intellectual grasp of biblical doctrine and failed to help disciples walk in step with the Spirit at work or school on a Monday morning. Catechesis as originally practised was specific about helping candidates face up to the struggles of temptation, breaking bad habits and vices and tackling those aspects of the surrounding culture that must be resisted. In our context we need to be learning and helping each other to cooperate with the Spirit in getting rid of the baggage we carry—the household

idols of our culture—such as consumerism and greed, workaholism, individualism, prejudicial divisions of all kinds, relativism, the pursuit of power, the cult of celebrity and the sexualisation of every part of life.[37]

3. **The process of catechesis makes it clear to new disciples that they are joining a countercultural community.** They know that in this community a different world view and behaviour are the norm—for example, that Christians are forgiving, generous and ready to make sacrifices, seek justice for all, see time as a gift and take Sabbath rest. New disciples are specifically prepared, trained and supported to live this new life. We need to think through how we can do this in Messy Church, and be more intentional about integrating people into our Christian community.

4. **Catechesis provides further evidence of the importance of Christian friends** who can take on the role of being mentors and models of Christian faith and life to new disciples. Such relationships require a huge commitment and investment of time over a period of perhaps three to five years to be effective, and for any individual to mentor more than one or two new disciples would probably be too much. If we want to see people growing as disciples, then we need to train and mobilise as many of our church members as possible to share in this mentoring work.[38]

Messy Churches also need to explore ways of keeping in touch with people by developing online aids to discipleship, utilising websites, email and social networking facilities such as Facebook and Twitter to build community and mentor families and individuals. For many who come to Messy Church, texting and social networking are probably the main ways they keep in touch with friends and family and plan their social lives. Electronic forms of communication therefore have great potential as tools for linking people up, sharing news and prayer requests and providing space to discuss and explore ideas and themes between the monthly meetings. The interactive aspect also fits well with Messy Church's ethos. However, it will require someone on the local team who is keen and up to speed with the technology, and who has the time and creativity to keep feeding the network with fresh snippets of news, teasers for the next Messy Church, video clips, pictures, comments, status updates, prayers and provocative discussion starters to keep the virtual community active.[39]

5. **Catechesis makes clear the cost of discipleship.** Following Christ requires us to take up our cross, die to our old self and begin a new life. People in a selfish, individualistic society must be challenged to commit their lives to Christ, even if, like the rich young man, they may then decide to walk away. Messy Church must not shy away from presenting the challenge of the Christian life.

6. **Catechesis, with its different stages, shows us that there is great value in giving people opportunities to put down 'markers' on their journey,** so that they can see how far they have travelled. Baptism (and confirmation in some churches) is obviously an important marker on the discipleship road, but others could be devised to mark earlier and later stages in the journey. For example, families who have been attending Messy Church for a while could be invited to mark their first steps in following Jesus and discovering more about

him by stepping with bare feet in a tray of paint and walking along a length of paper to leave their footprints, cheered on by everyone. A short prayer could be said for them, and a family would present them with a suitable book or Bible to read together at home. With permission, photos and videos could be taken and posted on YouTube and Facebook as a record of the event. At a later stage, families could be invited to add drawings or photographs of themselves to a Messy Church album that is displayed at each meeting as a simple way of affirming that they belong to this community of people who are entrusting their lives into God's hands.

Catechesis and Vatican 2

Since Vatican 2, there have been important developments in catechesis in the Roman Catholic Church that have a bearing on disciple-making in the church community and in families.

The revised edition of the *General Directory for Catechesis*, published in 1997, introduced a radical new approach of whole community catechesis centred on the weekly Mass. This emphasises lifelong, participative, intergenerational learning and helps families to grow in discipleship:

158. Catechetical pedagogy will be effective to the extent that the Christian community becomes a point of concrete reference for the faith journey of individuals. This happens when the community is proposed as a source, locus and means of catechesis. Concretely, the community becomes a visible place of faith-witness. It provides for the formation of its members. It receives them as the family of God.

It constitutes itself as the living and permanent environment for growth in the faith.[40]

As part of this programme, at Mass each week a set of practical discussion questions is provided, similar to the idea of having discussion questions over the meal in Messy Church. However, I am surprised it was felt necessary to give adults and children different versions of the same question. Here is one example:

Adults: *What can I do this week to bring Christ to everyone that I meet?*

Children: *What is one thing I can do to show my friends that God loves them?*[41]

Surely a single question could have been devised for all ages to discuss together?

Further resources are being developed to support this initiative. Although it has been designed primarily with existing congregations in mind rather than non-churched families, it clearly shares a number of values with Messy Church, particularly the focus on intergenerational worship and helping families develop their faith at home.

For further thought and discussion:

✢ How countercultural does Messy Church (or your church) look and feel?
✢ To what extent does Messy Church (or your church) present the cost of discipleship and the challenges of the Christian faith?

Chapter 9

Intergenerational discipleship

Messy Church began with the aim of reaching families, and so deliberately set out to be an intergenerational form of church, but a strong argument can be made that intergenerational church should be the norm.

God has made us one in Christ. We all receive the gift of the same Spirit. We all have gifts to use for the building up of the body. These truths will be most fully experienced when we all come together, and less so when we split up into smaller groups by age, sex or IQ. Church meetings should therefore regularly bring together all the parts of the body of Christ—men, women and children of all ages, colours, backgrounds, intelligences, personality types and preferred learning styles. We are differently shaped living stones that God is building into a temple. If this is the way that God is building the church to his design, we should expect to find disciple-making happens more naturally in an intergenerational community than in age-segregated groups.

Classes for different age groups have their place in education, although most schools gather for assemblies of some kind, and older pupils now often work alongside younger children to benefit both. In the church we have tended to assume that it is best to send the children out to age-segregated groups, largely because of the notion that young minds cannot understand more complex concepts, but discipleship, as we have seen, is about much more than being able to grasp concepts through formal teaching, and the spirituality of children can often go deeper than that of adults.

For thousands of years young people were educated and prepared for life mainly, if not exclusively, through socialisation in the context of the extended family and the local tribe or community, and not in age-segregated classes. Jewish and Christian faith and practice were largely passed on in this way, supplemented by some age-specific teaching.

Jesus has little time for those who set themselves up as teachers. In Matthew 23 he condemns the teachers of the law and the Pharisees for their hypocrisy: their strict teaching and yet wrong behaviour. Jesus insists his followers should not presume to be called teachers or rabbis. They should remember that they are all learners together with one teacher, the Messiah.

Historically, however, the church has replicated the old model, replacing the apostles, who were appointed to pass on the teaching of the Messiah to the first generation of the church, with overseers, pastor-teachers and later a professional class of ministers and clergy. People sit in rows in church buildings, facing the front, as if in a lecture theatre, like vessels waiting to be filled with knowledge by an expert, to be told what they should believe and how they should behave. In fact, we should be 'competent to instruct one another' (Romans 15:14), encouraging each other (2 Corinthians 13:11; 1 Thessalonians 5:11; Hebrews 3:13), correcting each other (Galatians 6:1–3), taking care not to trip one another up (Romans 14:13), serving one another (Galatians 5:13), bearing with one another (Ephesians 4:2), forgiving one another (Ephesians 4:32), bringing scriptures to one another (Ephesians 5:19), teaching and admonishing one another (Colossians 3:16), confessing our sins to each other (James 5:16) and loving one another (1 John).

The church is intended to be a community in which we hear and receive God's Word and the sacraments, and learn from one another through non-formal means and socialisation. However, the default setting for learning in most churches is formal, unidirectional and hierarchical. We urgently need to rediscover how to be an all-age disciple-making community, while recognising that it can sometimes be helpful for sub-groups of the church to meet for specific learning.

Most discipleship courses and materials are designed for adults, and a typical session is built around a presentation (often on DVD), followed by group discussion. There is a need for more interactive intergenerational material for use in Messy Church and other settings where adults and children learn together.

The view that intergenerational church should be our default setting is supported by the findings of research conducted in the United States, which compared children who had taken part in all-age worship with those who had not. The results show a number of differences between the two groups of children, most significantly in the area of prayer:

Children in the intergenerational (IG) group referred to prayer significantly more times in their interviews than did the children from non-IG settings. And in defining the concept of knowing God, more IG children in this sample gave relational descriptions of that concept than did non-IG children. In general, though both groups of children gave profound and eloquent testimony to their relationships with God, the IG children in this sample were more aware of their relationship with God, that is, more of them spoke more often and more reciprocally of that relationship.[42]

It would be interesting to do a similar study of the impact participation in an intergenerational church community has on adult disciples and their spiritual growth. A number of elderly people in their 90s love coming to our Messy Church every month, even though they do not have grandchildren or other family members attending the session. They find joy and encouragement from joining with all the generations, despite Messy Church being utterly different from the traditional style of worship that they have been accustomed to throughout their lives.

I firmly believe that the intergenerational approach is one of the key strengths of Messy Church, but I know of Messy Churches where the all-age aspect is sadly underplayed and parents are allowed to sit and chat while the children go off to do the crafts, listen to the Bible story and sing the song. Frankly, this is not Messy Church. They are unlikely to make disciples unless the leaders take on board the need to build relationships and work with the adults and the children together.

Messy Church, when done properly, is certainly not 'Church Lite'. Baptisms and Holy Communion can and do take place in Messy Church. The latter can be particularly moving when the bread has been baked that afternoon, the plate, cup and cloth decorated and the worship area lined with paintings by the congregation, as in a Messy Eucharist that took place at Portsmouth Cathedral. Messy Church has been shown to work perfectly well in churches with a more sacramental tradition. Messy Church at All Saints, Ladner, in Vancouver, Canada, for instance, includes the Eucharist every month.

At the Messy Church Round Table for Regional Coordinators in September 2007, Michael Moynagh, Director of Research for Fresh Expressions, identified making disciples as the key formational challenge facing the Fresh Expressions movement. I agree; it is the key challenge facing the whole Church. Moynagh went on to express doubt as to whether all aspects of discipleship could be covered in an all-age context such as Messy Church. He felt that some age-segregated learning would inevitably be needed.

It is encouraging to see Messy Churches using Alpha and other courses and small groups for adults in appropriate contexts. However, having explored the discipleship journey, how we learn through different modes, how disciples were made in the past, Macleod's manifesto for community discipleship and the research on the impact of intergenerational worship on children, I believe there are lots of good reasons why age-segregated discipleship groups are not necessarily the best way to go. I believe we should persevere with intentional intergenerational disciple-making in our Messy Churches and see how God makes us grow as disciples together.

For further thought and discussion:

✣ In your experience, do you think we learn more in church from the preacher or from one another?

✣ How should being a member of a church community help us to live as disciples?

Chapter 10

Discipleship and faith at home

Most parents feel a strong sense of responsibility for their children's upbringing. They will often acknowledge that there is a spiritual and moral dimension to this and admit they need help with this aspect. Supporting parents in the tough vocation of bringing up children and the responsibility of nurturing their faith and spirituality was identified as being important from quite early on in our discussions about discipleship and Messy Church. A member of the BRF Barnabas team leads on this area, and there is a dedicated website with research, advice and resources.[43]

Many parents feel ill-equipped, especially when it comes to nurturing a child's spirituality. An unhelpful legacy of several generations of religious teaching in schools and Sunday schools, and the more recent development of dedicated children's work and youth groups in churches, is that the church has been seen to be saying to parents, 'We're the experts; you can leave the spiritual formation of your children to us.' As a result, several generations of parents have been deskilled when it comes to nurturing their children's faith.

I know from my own childhood experience and from talking to others that in the homes of many families who regularly attend church services no prayers are ever said, the Bible gathers dust on the shelf, God is rarely if ever mentioned, and one would be hard-pushed to find any evidence of a Christian household.[44] At Messy Church training sessions, participants are often asked, 'Put your hand up if you were brought up in a Christian home.' Hands go up, and then the follow-up question is: 'How do you know?' Often the best answers people can come up with are: 'Because we went to church,' or, 'We were made to go to Sunday school.'

For many people, the almost complete absence of any overt Christian faith at home means that even churchgoing parents feel nonplussed when their children ask awkward questions about life, the universe and everything. Non-churched parents at Messy Church often express a similar feeling of anxiety and even guilt about this, and give this as a reason for bringing their children to Messy Church.

Messy Church certainly does not claim to give them all the answers, but we do want to encourage parents to take back the responsibility for the spiritual formation of their children by equipping them to explore faith and grow in discipleship along with their children. Families require support in order to learn the skills they need to live the Christian life and to pass those skills on to future generations.

As a gentle, unthreatening encouragement of faith at home, many Messy Churches produce take-home sheets with suggested extra activities for families to extend the theme explored at the monthly session. There might be a craft or messy experiment to do together, a prayer to use or a question to discuss linked to a Bible passage. In addition, many of the craft items made at Messy Church are meant to be taken home as a reminder of the Bible theme or story. It is good if at least one of these crafts each month involves making something that can be used at home, for example a prayer cube that could be rolled to choose a different person or topic to pray for each day.

These are obviously small steps on a steep learning curve, but over the months, families can gradually become more accustomed to the idea of bringing prayer and discussion about God into their daily lives. It is another area where the positive example and gentle encouragement of the Messy Church team and Christian families acting as friendly mentors will make a huge difference. It will be vital to do some learning about faith at home with the team first, since even lifelong churchgoers may have had little or no experience of this.

For further thought and discussion:

✣ Were you brought up in a Christian home? How do you know?

Conclusion

This is what the kingdom of God is like. A man scatters seed on the ground. Night and day, whether he sleeps or gets up, the seed sprouts and grows, though he does not know how. All by itself the soil produces grain—first the stalk, then the head, then the full kernel in the head. As soon as the grain is ripe, he puts the sickle to it, because the harvest has come.

MARK 4:26–29

God is evidently at work in the Messy Church movement. Adults and children are journeying towards God, coming to faith and growing as disciples. It is a form of Christian community with potential to model discipleship and nurture new disciples, less through traditional and formal ways of learning (although there are still opportunities for this) and more through non-formal learning and socialisation—an immersive learning experience.

Making disciples should ideally involve all three modes of learning: formal, non-formal and socialisation. The church has tended to put more emphasis on formal learning through sermons and courses, forgetting that the other two modes of learning are constantly impacting the development of our world view and how we live our lives. Messy Church, with its experiential and community-focused approach, is strong in these areas, and we are rediscovering important insights into disciple-making that are worth sharing with the wider church.

In Jesus' parable quoted on the previous page, the farmer scatters the seed on the ground, planting the kingdom in a specific context. Sowing the kingdom and **growing disciples in Messy Church requires contextualisation**. Like Vincent Donovan in his mission to the Masai, we are rediscovering our faith through Messy Church, experimenting, taking time to build relationships, rediscovering a community approach to discipleship and seeking to develop forms of church that are culturally appropriate to the people who are responding to God. What works and is needed will differ from place to place. Some Messy Churches will develop a variety of second meetings and extra courses; others will focus on one monthly session. Ideas, resources and good practice can be shared through the Messy Church network and website, while emphasising that there is no one-size-fits-all discipleship programme.

Like the seed sprouting in the parable, **making disciples takes time**, probably years, so we should not expect to see quick results in Messy Churches that have been running for only a few months or even a couple of years. As George Lings argues, just as you do not expect a child to be as mature as an adult, but still consider them fully human and assess them alongside their peers, so any assessment of fresh expressions of church, including Messy Churches, must take into account their youthfulness.[45] We need to tread gently among these seedlings, and resist the temptation to keep pulling them up to check if they are growing. Patience and perseverance are required.

Like the farmer, **the team leading Messy Church has a vital role**. Time and resources need to be invested in the training of team members. This will give them greater confidence to play their part in making disciples by intentionally modelling Christian faith, making the most of the craft time to listen and talk informally about the gospel and the ups and downs of life, building genuine relationships, and being prepared to give time to encouraging and mentoring families over an extended period, probably several years. Materials to help inspire new teams and assist existing teams in thinking through issues such as being all-age, hospitality, creativity, context, discipleship and growth are provided on the Messy Church DVD, with further resources and notes on the website.[46]

Team leaders should also pray and think about inviting one or two people who are not yet committed Christians to become CRB-checked, join the team and take on specific responsibilities and tasks at Messy Church. This not only helps to blur the distinction between 'us and them', the hosts and the guests, making Messy Church more of a genuine congregation, but it also builds friendship and trust, and gives individuals what can often prove to be a life-changing experience of faith and prayer in action.

At the Messy Church Round Table in 2009, someone posed an important question regarding the team that leads a Messy Church: 'Can a group of people that belong to Sunday church create and lead a primary place of belonging for those who attend on a weekday?' Our experience of Messy Church suggests that the answer is 'Yes', but the team members need to be devoted to Messy Church, just like ministers, clergy and other lay leaders who have to be fully committed to serving and worshipping in multiple congregations. As Vicar, I currently lead and belong to four entirely different Sunday congregations, plus Messy Church midweek once a month, but I do feel I am a committed member of them all.

The apostle Paul's deep commitment to all the young churches he writes to is a challenge: 'Because we loved you so much, we were delighted to share with you not only the gospel of God but our lives as well' (1 Thessalonians 2:8). Messy Church needs to be taken as seriously as this. It requires this level of commitment from the team. Team members should be encouraged to see Messy Church as their church, not just another activity with which they help out. The time they give to leading at Messy Church should be regarded as their main way of serving the local church, not simply one among many other church responsibilities. We certainly have some way to go before our team's sense of belonging to Messy Church is as strong as this, but it is the right aspiration to have, if we are to free up more time and energy for keeping in touch with families and building relationships.

Finally, like the farmer, who with joy and relief sees the seed sprouting and growing, we happily admit that **we do not understand this wonderful growth** we observe taking place through Messy Church. Thank God that the harvest is not ultimately dependent on our messy efforts, on our getting all our relationships, conversations, behaviour, theology and cultural analysis exactly right every time! Thank God for the creative work of the Holy Spirit, who takes all our endeavours and amazes us by using them to draw people to Jesus and grow disciples. 'So neither the one who plants nor the one who waters is anything, but only God, who makes things grow' (1 Corinthians 3:7).

Summary of main recommendations

✣ It is vital that we give families a warm welcome when they come to Messy Church for the first time, and do all we can to help them develop a sense of belonging over the first few months. We should accept all people just as they are, with all their faults and baggage, as a sign of God's grace, as Jesus did. Let them be with us and be blessed, and have a taste of belonging to God's kingdom community. (pp. 18 and 66)

✣ Research shows that it usually takes between one and five years for someone to become a Christian. It is therefore unrealistic to expect a Messy Church to prove its effectiveness by producing lots of new Christians after only a year or two. This has important implications for how Messy Church is evaluated by church councils and denominations, especially when there are decisions to be made about staffing and funding. A new Messy Church will require investment in leaders and resources for longer than a couple of years if it is to have a chance of bearing fruit. (p. 21)

✣ Personal invitation and being brought along by someone you know and trust is vital for introducing people into a new environment. (p. 22)

✣ Encouraging newcomers to take on tasks and responsibilities is important, because they feel needed and this reinforces their sense of belonging. (pp. 22–23)

✣ More resources for exploring Christian faith that are specifically designed for those who have little or no church background are needed, including material that can be used by adults and children together. (p. 23)

✣ People at different stages on the journey of faith require different kinds of input, support and encouragement at each stage to keep moving on towards believing and behaving: initially welcome, friendship and a positive experience of the church community, then sharing the good news and helping with questions, and later mentoring as disciples. (pp. 32–34)

✢ Making disciples who will be able to adapt to living as Christians in a rapidly changing world requires all three modes of learning: formal, non-formal and socialisation. Inherited church puts more emphasis on formal, unidirectional and hierarchical learning, forgetting that the other two modes of learning have a major impact on the development of our world view and how we live our lives. Disciple-making requires mentoring and coaching, learning through experience, and being sent out on mission. Time and resources need to be invested in the training and development of the team members so that they can rediscover how to be an all-age, all-embracing, disciple-making community. Team members need confidence to play their part by intentionally modelling Christian faith, making the most of the craft time to listen and talk informally about the gospel, building genuine relationships and being prepared to give time to encouraging and mentoring families over an extended period. (pp. 38–39, 66, 107, 115 and 116)

✢ Messy Church should develop an intentional socialisation programme of imaginative, participative all-age celebrations at major festivals so that we learn to live in a rhythm of reviewing, renewing and passing on the faith. Alongside this we need to help families develop a weekly Sabbath rhythm, make links between faith and everyday life, and practise their faith at home. (pp. 47 and 113)

✢ We should recognise that disciples are made in a community with the risen Christ at the centre as our teacher and model. Are we intentionally operating in our Messy Church community in such a way that disciple-making happens? (pp. 82–83)

✤ Good relationships with one another are vital, and require time and commitment to develop. There must be patience, forgiveness and encouragement. We need to focus on learning how to love and serve one another as the universally recognised sign that we are Christ's disciples. (pp. 66–67)

✤ Those who are leaders must be prepared to give of themselves to people, and to have their lives on show as humble, imperfect models of discipleship. Ideally, team members should be fully committed to Messy Church as their church, and this should be their main way of serving, not simply one among many church responsibilities. (pp. 67 and 117)

✤ As an intergenerational community we must welcome and bless the lowest and the least and learn what it means to have a childlike relationship with the Lord. (p. 67)

✤ Young Messy Churches and their leaders require a great deal of support and encouragement if they are to help people on their journey into faith and discipleship. It will be important for Messy Churches to feel that they are loved, cared for and prayed for. Members of the BRF Messy Church Team will need to make visits to Messy Churches and provide support in the form of consultation, training and resources. (p. 77)

✤ Messy Church is rediscovering a community approach to discipleship and seeking to develop forms of church that are culturally appropriate. What is needed will differ from place to place. Some Messy Churches will develop a variety of second meetings and extra courses; others will continue to focus on one monthly session. (p. 116)

✦ Ideas, resources and good practice need to be shared through the Messy Church network and website, while emphasising that there is no one-size-fits-all discipleship programme. (p. 116)

✦ Leaders should invite one or two people who are not yet committed Christians to join the team and take on specific responsibilities, roles and tasks. This can often prove to be a life-changing experience for them. (p. 117)

✦ Remember that this is God's work. We certainly do not have everything sussed—it is messy. Go for it, see what God does, and rejoice! (p. 118)

Endnotes

1. For the background to Messy Church, see Lucy Moore, *Messy Church* (BRF, 2006) and Lucy Moore, *Messy Church 2* (BRF, 2008).
2. *Expressions: The DVD—1: Stories of Church for a Changing Culture* (Church House Publishing, 2006).
3. 'Discipleship input': www.messychurch.org.uk/pages/6179.htm. The baptism took place on 18 September 2011. See 'Messy Church leads to baptisms': www.messychurch.org.uk/pages/6395.htm.
4. Nick Spencer, *Beyond the Fringe: Researching a Spiritual Age* (Cliff College Publishing, 2005) and Nick Spencer, *Beyond Belief?* (The London Institute for Contemporary Christianity, 2003).
5. James F. Engel and Wilbert H. Norton, *What's Gone Wrong With the Harvest?: A Communication Strategy for the Church and World Evangelism* (Zondervan, 1975). The scale has often been modified to show a different number of stages.
6. John Finney in *Finding Faith Today* (Bible Society, 1992), pp. 22–25, gave the average time as four years. More recent research by Dave Bennett finds an average of two to three years. See 'A Study of How Adults Become Christians with Special Reference to the Personal Involvement of Individual Christians' (a dissertation submitted in part fulfilment of the requirements for the Degree of MA in Evangelism Studies, University of Sheffield, at Cliff College, 2003), pp. 31–33: www.bridge-builders.net/current/dissertation/dissertation_whole.doc.
7. The Journeys course was devised by Rob Harley and published by Great Journeys in 2003 (www.greatjourneys.org). Similar DVD-based courses suitable for those with little or no church background are Start (www.start-cpas.org.uk) and Puzzling Questions by Paul Griffiths (Monarch, 2012).
8. www.thegraymatrix.info. I have adapted Gray's diagram by numbering the quadrants for ease of reference and suggesting my own labels for them.
9. For a provocative critique see Alan Hirsch, *The Forgotten Ways: Reactivating the Missional Church* (Brazos Press, 2006).

10. 'Messy Church Crafts Colourful Alternative Sundays', *The Times*, 19 May 2012, p. 85.
11. Email to the author, 28 May 2012.
12. Judy Paulsen, work in progress for D. Min. in Missional Leadership at Fuller Theological Seminary, USA.
13. This remark was made at the National Children's Advisors' Conference held in Hertfordshire in April 2011.
14. From work by Professor Ted Ward of Michigan University, outlined in a paper by Bob Hopkins, 'Towards Pioneer Missional Leadership (For Mission-Shaped Church)', May 2003: www.acpi.org.uk/Joomla/index.php?option=com_content&task=view&id=62&Itemid=65.
15. On learning and music see John V. Witvliet, 'Afterword. Mr Holland's Advice: A Call to Immersive Cross-Disciplinary Learning' in Jeremy S. Begbie and Steven R. Guthrie (eds), *Resonant Witness: Conversations Between Music and Theology* (Eerdmans, 2011), pp. 456–57.
16. Christopher J.H. Wright, *The Mission of God's People: A Biblical Theology of the Church's Mission* (Zondervan, 2010), especially pp. 63–81 on Abraham.
17. See David Wenham, *Parables of Jesus: Pictures of Revolution* (Hodder and Stoughton, 1989).
18. It is not clear in the Gospels if all new followers of Jesus were baptised, or if this requirement was only for those who had not previously been baptised by John the Baptist. The latter might seem logical, since Jesus himself was also baptised by John, but in Acts 19:1–7 a dozen disciples in Ephesus who have previously received 'John's baptism' are 'baptised into the name of Jesus' by Paul.
19. A number of books and discipleship courses take up the apprenticeship model, e.g. the Lifeshapes course described in Mike Breen and Steve Cockram, *Building a Discipling Culture* (3DM, 2009), and James Bryan Smith's 'The Apprentice Series' resources (www.apprenticeofjesus.org).
20. Bob Hopkins, 'Moving from Courses to Coaching': www.acpi.org.uk/Joomla/index.php?option=com_content&task=view&id=122&Itemid=65.

21. Vincent J. Donovan, *Christianity Rediscovered: An Epistle from the Masai* (SCM, 1982), p. 84.
22. Christopher J.H. Wright, *The Mission of God's People*, p. 73.
23. Graham Cray, *Disciples & Citizens: A Vision for Distinctive Living* (IVP, 2007), p. 126.
24. John R.W. Stott, *The Message of Acts* (IVP, 1990), p. 305, footnote 42.
25. Alan Kreider, *The Change of Conversion and the Origin of Christendom* (Wipf and Stock, 2006), p. 21.
26. Bob Hopkins, 'Introduction and Background to Cell Church': www. acpi.org.uk/Joomla/index.php?option=com_content&task=view&id =53&Itemid=65.
27. The London Institute for Contemporary Christianity has addressed this issue extensively. See Mark Greene and Tracey Cotterell (eds), *Let My People Grow: Making Disciples Who Make a Difference in Today's World* (Authentic Media, 2006).
28. George Lings, *Seven Sacred Spaces: Encountering Community Life in Christ, Encounters on the Edge* no. 43 (The Sheffield Centre, 2009).
29. George Lings, *Seven Sacred Spaces: Encountering Community Life in Christ, Encounters on the Edge* no. 43, p. 23.
30. Cards are already available for use in the home: http://eatathomecooks. com/2010/09/table-talk-cards-using-dinner-as-opportunity-to-connect-with-kids.html.
31. Claire Dalpra, 'Happening Upon the Three Spaces', *Models of Engagement*: Research Bulletin no. 7 (The Sheffield Centre, winter 2010/11), p. 4.
32. Duncan Macleod, *Mission Stories: A Six-Part Guide to the Church in Mission* (2010), available at www.faithstories.org.au.
33. From Duncan Macleod's Sydney lecture handout, 'Gospel Questions for Gospel People', on 18 August 2011, and Macleod's blog entry: www.postkiwi.com/2011/messy-ministry-context-in-sydney.
34. The Five Marks of Mission were developed by the Anglican Consultative Council between 1984 and 1990, and provide churches with a checklist for mission activities. They are: to proclaim the Good News of the Kingdom; to teach, baptise and

nurture new believers; to respond to human need by loving service; to seek to transform unjust structures of society; to strive to safeguard the integrity of creation and sustain and renew the life of the earth.

35. For information on toilet twinning, see www.toilettwinning.org.

36. Alan Kreider, *The Change of Conversion and the Origin of Christendom*, pp. 1–32.

37. On these themes, see Graham Cray, *Disciples & Citizens*, pp. 53–95.

38. CPAS has produced *Mentoring Matters*, a resource to help churches identify, equip and resource church-based mentors. See www.cpas.org.uk/church-resources/mentoring-matters.

39. Richard Moy and Anna Drew, *Leadership and Social Networking: Updating Your Ministry Status* (Grove Books, 2011).

40. Congregation for the Clergy, *General Directory for Catechesis* (Catholic Truth Society, 1997), also available online at: www.vatican.va/roman_curia/congregations/cclergy/documents/rc_con_ccatheduc_doc_17041998_directory-for-catechesis_en.html.

41. www.wholecommunitycatechesis.com

42. Holly Catterton Allen, 'A Qualitative Study Exploring the Similarities and Differences of the Spirituality of Children in Intergenerational and Non-Intergenerational Christian Contexts' (pp. 184–94). Doctoral dissertation, Talbot School of Theology, Biola University, La Mirada, CA, 2002.

43. www.faithinhomes.org.uk/

44. See the findings of the 'Faith at Home Questionnaire Summary' at www.brf.uk.net/pdfs/faithathome_responses.pdf/.

45. George Lings, 'Evaluating Fresh Expressions of Church as Well as Our Thinking About Them', 20 October 2010 (unpublished paper).

46. *Messy Church—the DVD* (BRF, 2011).